Beautiful Blankets, Afghans and Throws

Beautiful Blankets, Afghans and Throws

40 Blocks and Stitch Patterns to Crochet

Leonie Morgan

Search Press

A QUARTO BOOK

Published in 2017 by
Search Press Ltd
Wellwood
North Farm Road
Tunbridge Wells
Kent TN2 3DR

ISBN: 978-1-78221-543-1

Conceived, designed and produced by
Quarto Publishing plc
The Old Brewery
6 Blundell Street
London N7 9BH
www.quartoknows.com

QUAR.STPA

Editors: Lily de Gatacre, Michelle Pickering
Senior art editor: Emma Clayton
Layout designer: Jo Bettles
Photographers: Nicki Dowey, Phil Wilkins
Pattern checker: Therese Chynoweth
Chart illustrations: Kuo Kang Chen
Editorial assistant: Danielle Watt
Designer: Martina Calvio
Art director: Caroline Guest
Creative director: Moira Clinch
Publisher: Sam Warrington

Colour separation by PICA Digital Pte Ltd,
Singapore

Printed by 1010 Printing International Ltd,
China

Contents

Edgings 100

Techniques 110

Welcome

Turning a strand of yarn into a crochet design is always a journey of exploration for me. I never quite know what I'll make until my hands begin to move. Sometimes I have a vague idea in mind before I start to crochet, but more often it's a complete mystery to me. My hands move, stitches appear and before long I've designed something – not always perfect to start with, but something that I can tweak and develop into a pattern.

My favourite designs are patterns that can be used for afghans, be they square blocks or row-by-row designs. Afghans are my favourite sort of project to have on the go in my yarn basket. Bit by bit, the squares add up to a tottering pile of colourful loveliness, or the afghan steadily grows as each row is added. There is nothing more satisfying in the crochet world (besides the obvious deliciousness of buying new yarn) than weaving in the last horrid yarn end of an afghan you've made. Nestling under the freshly made and gorgeous crochet blanket gives you a feeling of very smug satisfaction!

In this book I've gathered 40 fab patterns to crochet into afghans. Half of the designs are block patterns and the other half are row-by-row patterns, so you have a choice of what sort of afghan to make. For each of the designs, you will find yarn quantities for making blankets in three different sizes at the back of the book, so you can get crocheting straightaway.

I hope this book will give you lots of happy crocheting time and inspiration, and help you to experience the wonderful feeling of completing an afghan of your own.

Happy Hooking!

Leonie Morgan

About This Book

This book is an eye-catching resource of afghan patterns for you to crochet. As well as the 40 main designs, there are 12 edging patterns to give your afghan the perfect finish. At the end of the book you will find information on techniques and yarn quantities.

Edgings, pages 100–109

There are 12 edging designs to help you finish your afghan perfectly.

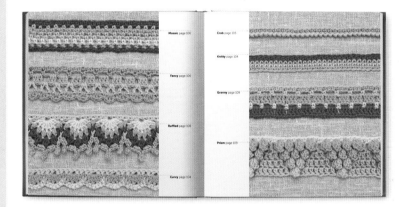

Techniques, pages 110–123

An illustrated, comprehensive and concise guide provides everything you need to know to get started crocheting the afghans. At the end of the book you will also find a list of yarn quantities for making three different sizes of afghan using each of the main designs.

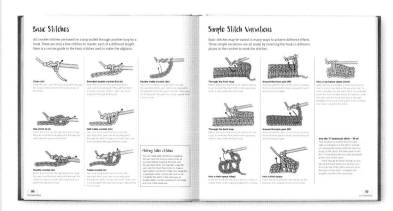

Afghan Collection, pages 8–99

At the heart of this book are the 40 afghan designs. With written patterns, charts and clear photographs taking you through each design, you will want to start crocheting right away.

■ Five of the patterns have been made into full-size finished afghans to inspire you.

■ Instructions for any special stitches used in each design are provided alongside the pattern.

Skill level gives a rough guide to difficulty:
1 = easy
2 = intermediate
3 = advanced

Hook size and type of yarn used to make the sample shown.

Half of the patterns are block designs and half are row-by-row designs.

Tension information is provided as either the finished size of a single block or the number of stitches and rows to a given size.

Additional information lists any special techniques used and whether the design is reversible (the same on both sides).

List of yarn colours for each design. Quantities are provided for making a single block or the full-size afghan shown. Refer also to page 124 for yarn quantities for three different sizes of afghan.

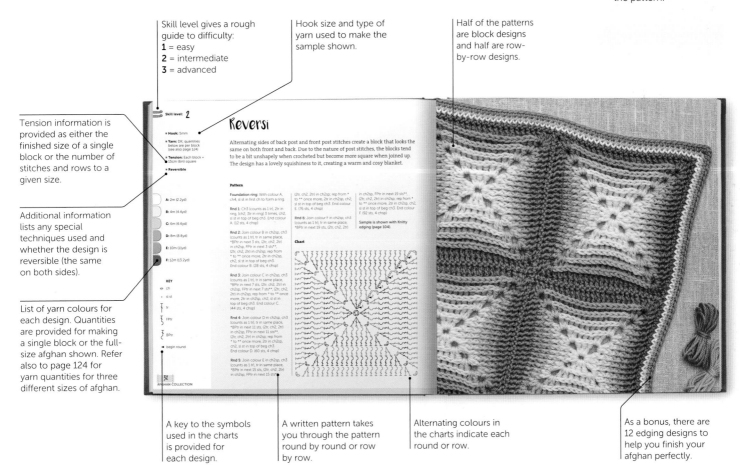

A key to the symbols used in the charts is provided for each design.

A written pattern takes you through the pattern round by round or row by row.

Alternating colours in the charts indicate each round or row.

As a bonus, there are 12 edging designs to help you finish your afghan perfectly.

Afghan Collection

On the following pages you will find 40 bright and colourful afghan patterns. Split into 20 block designs and 20 row-by-row designs, and ranging from beginner to advanced level, there is plenty to choose from. Check page 124 for yarn quantities for three different sizes of afghan for each pattern.

- **Hook:** 5mm
- **Yarn:** DK (see page 124 for quantities)
- **Tension:** 14 sts and 13 rows in pattern = 10cm (4in) square

A

B

C

D

E

F

G

H

KEY

o   ch
+   dc
⊤   htr
⊤   tr
   bobble
◄   begin row

Bobble Along

Bands of aligned and staggered bobbles surrounded by rows of simple stitches create a warm and tactile afghan. The dense stitching also makes this pattern especially suitable for baby blankets.

Pattern

Foundation row: With colour A, ch a multiple of 2 + 2 + 3 turning ch.

Row 1 (RS): Beg in 5th ch from hook (first ch3 counts as 1 tr), tr in each ch to end. End colour A. Turn.

Row 2 (WS): Join colour B, ch1, dc in each st to end. End colour B. Turn.

Row 3: Join colour C, ch2 (counts as 1 htr), htr in each st to end. End colour C. Turn.

Row 4: Repeat row 2 using colour D. End colour D. Turn.

Row 5: Repeat row 2 using colour E. Do not end colour E. Turn.

Row 6: Ch1, dc in first st, [dc in next st, BO in next st] to last st, dc in last st. End colour E. Turn.

Row 7: Repeat row 2 using colour F. Do not end colour F. Turn.

Row 8: Ch1, dc in first st, [BO in next st, dc in next st] to last st, dc in last st. End colour F. Turn.

Rows 9 + 10: Repeat rows 5 + 6 using colour G. End colour G. Turn.

Rows 11 + 12: Repeat rows 7 + 8 using colour H. End colour H. Do not turn.

Row 13: Join colour D in first st of last row and repeat row 2. End colour D. Turn.

Row 14: Repeat row 3 using colour C. End colour C. Turn.

Row 15: Repeat row 2 using colour B. End colour B. Turn.

Row 16: Join colour A, ch3 (counts as 1 tr), tr in each st to end. End colour A. Turn.

Row 17: Repeat row 5 using colour G. End colour G. Turn.

Rows 18 + 19: Repeat rows 7 + 8 using colour F. End colour F. Turn.

Rows 20 + 21: Repeat rows 18 + 19 using colour C. End colour C. Turn.

Rows 22 + 23: Repeat rows 18 + 19 using colour H. End colour H. Do not turn.

Row 24: Join colour G in first st of last row and repeat row 2. Turn.

Row 25: Repeat row 16 using colour A. End colour A. Turn.

Repeat rows 2–25 until fabric is the desired length.

Chart

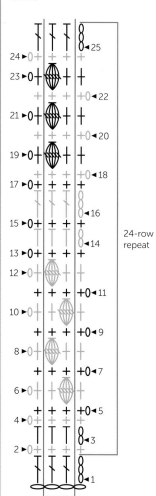

24-row repeat

2-st repeat

SPECIAL STITCH

Bobble (BO):
Work 5tr in place indicated but omit final yo of each tr, yo and pull through all 6 loops on hook.

Skill level: 3

- **Hook:** 5mm
- **Yarn:** DK (see page 124 for quantities)
- **Tension:** 9 sts and 8 rows = 10cm (4in) square

A
B
C
D
E
F
G
H

KEY

○	ch
+	dc
T	htr
⋏	htr2tog
	beg CL
	CL
	bead stitch
♡	surface crochet heart
◄	begin row

Band of Hearts

Rows of half treble crochet and cluster stitches create a soft, squidgy afghan, while bands of surface crochet and bead stitch hearts add interest and colour.

Pattern

Foundation row: With colour A, loosely ch a multiple of 4 + 2 + 1 turning ch.

Row 1 (RS): Dc in 2nd ch from hook, htr in next ch, [htr2tog] to end, htr in last ch. End colour A. Turn.

Row 2 (WS): Join colour B, ch1, dc in first st, htr in next st, [htr2tog] to end, htr in last st. End colour B. Turn.

Row 3: Repeat row 2 using colour C. End colour C. Do not turn.

Row 4: Join colour D, beg CL in first st, *CL in each of next 2 sts, ch1, CL in each of next 2 sts; rep from * to last st, CL in last st. End colour D. Do not turn.

Surface crochet hearts: With RS facing, join colour E in first ch1sp on right-hand side of row 4, work surface crochet heart; rep in each ch1sp to end, alternating colours E and C. Turn.

Rows 5–7: Repeat row 2 using colour F, then colour G, then colour A.

Row 8: Repeat row 4 using colour D. End colour D. Do not turn.

Row 9: Join colour H, ch4 (counts as 1 tr, ch1), *skip 2 sts, (BS, ch1, BS)

in ch1sp, skip 2 sts**, ch3; rep from * to last 5 sts, rep from * to ** once, ch1, tr in last st. End colour H. Do not turn.

Row 10: Join colour D in 3rd ch of beg ch4 of row 9, ch1 and dc in same place, *working behind row 9 and into row 8: CL in next st, tr in next 2 sts, CL in next st; rep from * to last st, dc in last st of row 9. End colour D. Do not turn.

Row 11: Join colour D in first dc of last row, beg CL in first st, CL in each st to end. End colour D. Turn.

Rows 12–14: Repeat row 2 using colour A, then colour G, then colour F.

Row 15: Join colour D and repeat row 4. Do not turn.

Surface crochet hearts: With RS facing, join colour C in first ch1sp on right-hand side of row 15, work surface crochet heart; rep in each ch1sp to end, alternating colours C and E. Do not turn.

Row 16: Join colour A in first st of last row and repeat row 2. End colour A. Turn.

Repeat rows 2–16 until fabric is the desired length.

Chart

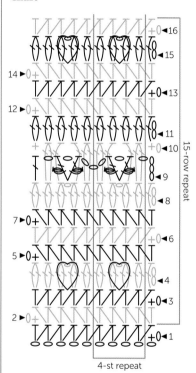

15-row repeat

4-st repeat

Surface crochet heart

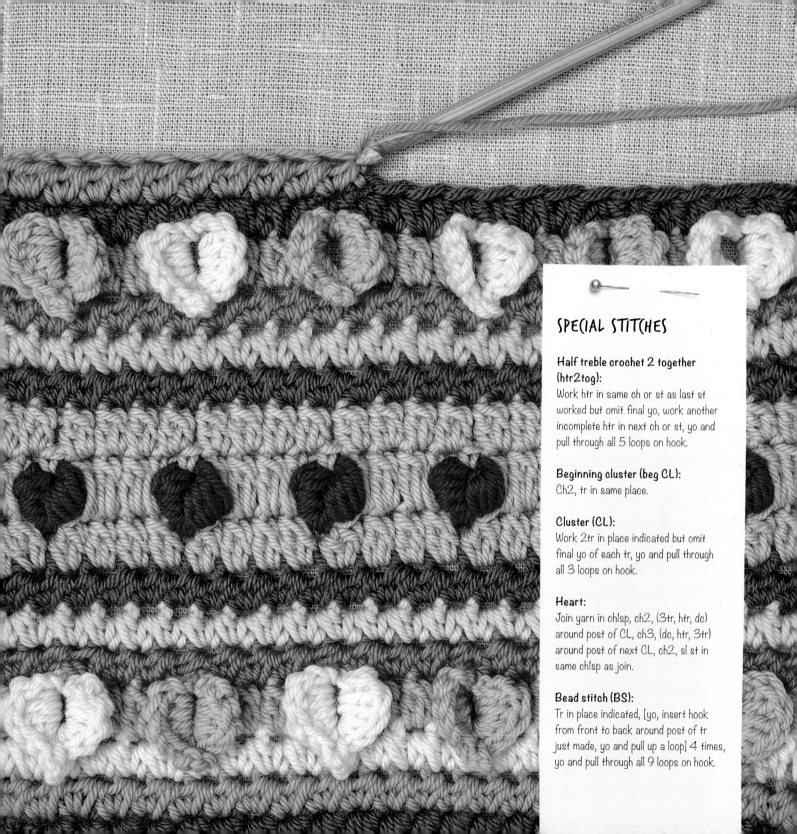

SPECIAL STITCHES

Half treble crochet 2 together (htr2tog):
Work htr in same ch or st as last st worked but omit final yo, work another incomplete htr in next ch or st, yo and pull through all 5 loops on hook.

Beginning cluster (beg CL):
Ch2, tr in same place.

Cluster (CL):
Work 2tr in place indicated but omit final yo of each tr, yo and pull through all 3 loops on hook.

Heart:
Join yarn in ch1sp, ch2, (3tr, htr, dc) around post of CL, ch3, (dc, htr, 3tr) around post of next CL, ch2, sl st in same ch1sp as join.

Bead stitch (BS):
Tr in place indicated, [yo, insert hook from front to back around post of tr just made, yo and pull up a loop] 4 times, yo and pull through all 9 loops on hook.

- **Hook:** 6mm
- **Yarn:** DK (see page 124 for quantities)
- **Tension:** 12 sts and 24 rows = 9cm (3½in) wide x 11cm (4¼in) high
- **Crochet technique:** Tapestry (page 119)
- **Reversible**

A

B

C

D

Baby Diamonds

Baby Diamonds is a tapestry crochet pattern, so the stitches are close fitting and create a thick, warm fabric. It has an almost woven texture that is perfect for babies and little baby fingers. For a neat finish, insert the hook under the carried strand of yarn when working the stitches, and join new colours at the start of the row.

Chart

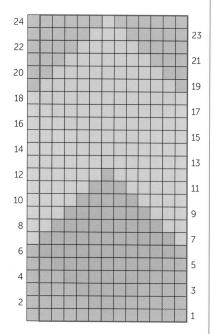

Pattern

Foundation row: With colour A, ch a multiple of 12 + 1 + 1 turning ch.

Working from chart: Start at the bottom right-hand corner of the chart and work in double crochet, beginning the first row in the 2nd ch from hook. Each square represents 1 stitch. Right-side rows are read from right to left and wrong-side rows are read from left to right. Remember to ch1 at the beginning of each row for a turning ch (this does not count as a stitch).

To change to a different colour: Join the new colour required at the beginning of the row, hold the new (or unused) colour along the top edge, and work double crochet over it until it is needed. To change from one colour to another, work to 1 stitch before the colour change. Begin this stitch normally, working to the last yarn over, then drop the current colour to the wrong side of the work, pick up the new colour and use it to complete the stitch.

Pattern repeat: The section highlighted in red on the chart is the pattern repeat. Repeat this section until you have 1 stitch remaining on right-side rows, then work the last stitch at the left edge of the chart. On wrong-side rows, work the first stitch, then repeat the highlighted section to the end of the row.

- **Hook:** 5mm
- **Yarn:** DK; quantities below are per block (see also page 124)
- **Tension:** Each block = 15cm (6in) square

A: 1.5m (1.7yd)

B: 2.5m (2.8yd)

C: 6.5m (7.2yd)

D: 13m (14.3yd)

E: 8m (8.8yd)

KEY

o	ch
•	sl st
+	dc
⊤	htr
⊤	tr
🖉	beg CL
🖉	CL
◄	begin round

Dazzling Daisy

This cheerful crochet block would look fantastic in lots of different colourways. The pattern has one round of cluster stitches but is otherwise an easy pattern. Try working the flowers in bright colours and the borders in a neutral colour, or you could work round 3 in a fluffier yarn for added texture.

Pattern

Foundation ring: With colour A, ch4, sl st in first ch to form a ring.

Rnd 1: Ch3 (counts as 1 tr), 11tr in ring, sl st in top of beg ch3. End colour A. (12 sts)

Rnd 2: Join colour B, ch5 (counts as 1 tr, ch2), [tr in next st, ch2] 11 times, sl st in 3rd ch of beg ch5. End colour B. (12 sts, 12 chsp)

Rnd 3: Join colour C in ch2sp, beg CL in same place, [ch3, CL in next ch2sp] 11 times, ch3, sl st in top of beg CL. End colour C. (12 CL, 12 chsp)

Rnd 4: Join colour D in ch3sp, ch1, [4dc in ch3sp] 12 times, sl st in first dc made. End colour D. (48 sts)

Rnd 5: Join colour E in first dc in any group of 4dc, ch3 (counts as 1 tr), *2tr in next st, ch2, 2tr in next st, tr in next st, htr in next st, dc in next 6 sts, htr in next st**, tr in next st; rep from * twice more, then from * to ** once, sl st in top of beg ch3. (56 sts, 4 chsp)

Rnd 6: Sl st in each st to corner ch2sp, ch3 (counts as 1 tr), (tr, ch2, 2tr) in same place, [tr in each st to next corner ch2sp, (2tr, ch2, 2tr) in ch2sp] 3 times, tr in each st to end,

sl st in top of beg ch3. End colour E. (72 sts, 4 chsp)

Rnd 7: Join colour D in ch2sp, ch1, [(dc, htr, dc) in ch2sp, dc in next 18 sts] 4 times, sl st in first dc made. End colour D. (84 sts)

Chart

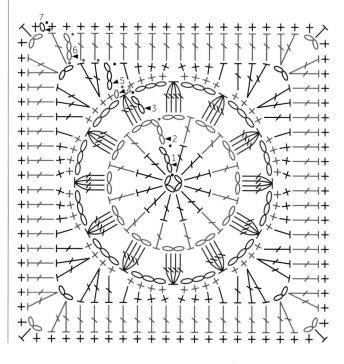

SPECIAL STITCHES

Beginning cluster (beg CL):
Ch2, work 3tr in place indicated but omit final yo of each tr, yo and pull through all 4 loops on hook.

Cluster (CL):
Work 4tr in place indicated but omit final yo of each tr, yo and pull through all 5 loops on hook.

- **Hook:** 5mm

- **Yarn:** DK; quantities below are per block (see also page 124)

- **Tension:** Each block = 15cm (6in) square

A: 1.5m (1.7yd)

B: 9.5m (10.4yd)

C: 2m (2.2yd)

D: 8m (8.8yd)

E: 3m (3.3yd)

F: 3.5m (3.9yd)

G: 4m (4.4yd)

KEY

o · ch

· sl st

+ dc

T htr

T̄ tr

◀ begin row or round

Granny's Corner

An alternative to the traditional granny square, this block is worked from corner to corner. This is another great stash-busting pattern, or you could use different colours for even-numbered rows and one neutral colour for odd-numbered rows. All rows and rounds are worked from the right side.

Pattern

Foundation ring: With colour A, ch4, sl st in first ch to form a ring.

Row 1: Ch3 (counts as 1 tr), (3tr, ch2, 4tr) in ring. End colour A. (8 sts, 1 chsp)

Row 2: Join colour B in first st of last row, ch1 and dc in same place, ch2, skip 3 sts, (dc, ch3, dc) in ch2sp, ch2, skip 3 sts, dc in last st. End colour B. (4 sts, 3 chsps)

Row 3: Join colour C in first st of last row, ch3 (counts as 1 tr), 3tr in ch2sp, (3tr, ch2, 3tr) in ch3sp, 3tr in ch2sp, tr in last st. End colour C. (14 sts, 1 chsp)

Chart

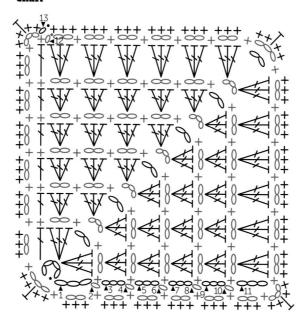

Row 4: Join colour B in first st of last row, ch1 and dc in same place, ch2, skip 3 sts, dc in gap before next st, ch2, skip 3 sts, (dc, ch3, dc) in ch2sp, ch2, skip 3 sts, dc in gap before next st, ch2, skip 3 sts, dc in last st. End colour B. (6 sts, 5 chsps)

Row 5: Join colour D in first st of last row, ch3 (counts as 1 tr), [3tr in next ch2sp] twice, (3tr, ch2, 3tr) in ch3sp, [3tr in next ch2sp] twice, tr in last st. End colour D. (20 sts, 1 chsp)

Row 6: Join colour B in first st of last row, ch1 and dc in same place, [ch2, skip 3 sts, dc in gap before next st] twice, ch2, skip 3 sts, (dc, ch3, dc) in ch2sp, [ch2, skip 3 sts, dc in gap before next st] twice, ch2, skip 3 sts, dc in last st. End colour B. (8 sts, 7 chsps)

Row 7: Join colour E in first st of last row, ch3 (counts as 1 tr), [3tr in next ch2sp] 3 times, (3tr, ch2, 3tr) in ch3sp, [3tr in next ch2sp] 3 times, tr in last st. End colour E. (26 sts, 1 chsp)

Row 8: Join colour B in first st of last row, ch1 and dc in same place, [ch2, skip 3 sts, dc in gap before next st] 3 times, ch2, skip 3 sts, (dc, ch3, dc) in ch2sp, [ch2, skip 3 sts, dc in gap before next st] 3 times, ch2, skip 3 sts, dc in last st. End colour B. (10 sts, 9 chsp)

Row 9: Join colour F in first st of last row, ch3 (counts as 1 tr), [3tr in next ch2sp] 4 times, (3tr, ch2, 3tr) in ch3sp, [3tr in next ch2sp] 4 times, tr in last st. End colour F. (32 sts, 1 chsp)

Row 10: Join colour B in first st of last row, ch1 and dc in same place, [ch2, skip 3 sts, dc in gap before next st] 4 times, ch2, skip 3 sts, (dc, ch3, dc) in ch2sp, [ch2, skip 3 sts, dc in gap before next st] 4 times, ch2, skip 3 sts, dc in last st. End colour B. (12 sts, 11 chsp)

Row 11: Join colour G in first st of last row, ch3 (counts as 1 tr), [3tr in next ch2sp] 5 times, (3tr, ch2, 3tr) in ch3sp, [3tr in next ch2sp] 5 times, tr in last st. End colour G. (38 sts, 1 chsp)

Edging

Rnd 12: Join colour B in last st made, ch1, (dc, ch3, dc) in same place, [ch2, dc in side of next dc along edge of block] 5 times, ch2, (dc, ch3, dc) in foundation ring, [ch2, dc in side of next dc along

edge of block] 5 times, ch2, (dc, ch3, dc) in top of first st on row 11, [ch2, skip 3 sts, dc in gap before next st] 5 times, ch2, (dc, ch3, dc) in ch2sp, [ch2, skip 3 sts, dc in gap before next st] 5 times, ch2, sl st in first dc made. End colour B. (28 sts, 28 chsp)

Rnd 13: Join colour D in ch3sp, ch1, *(2dc, htr, 2dc) in ch3sp, [3dc in next ch2sp] 6 times; rep from * 3 times more, sl st in first dc made. End colour D. (92 sts)

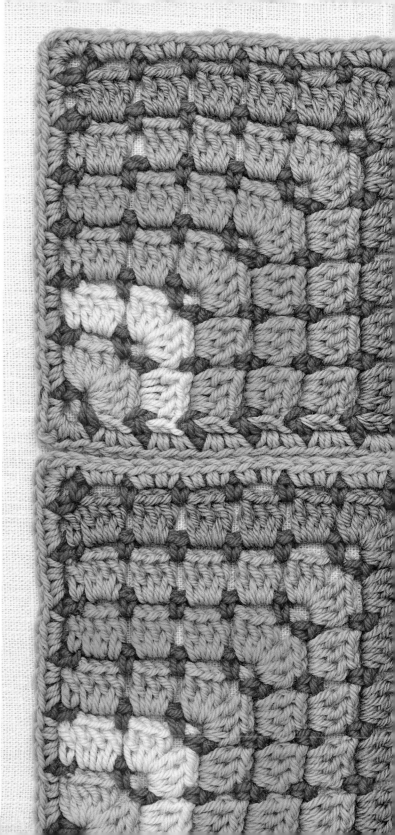

- **Hook:** 5mm

- **Yarn:** DK; quantities below are per block (see also page 124)

- **Tension:** Each block = 15cm (6in) square

- **Crochet technique:** Intarsia (page 119)

- **Reversible**

A: 13m (14.3yd)

B: 3m (3.3yd)

C: 2m (2.2yd)

D: 7m (7.7yd)

E: 7m (7.7yd)

Interrupted

This colourwork block is very easy to crochet. The stitches are close fitting, making it ideal for baby blankets. Try laying the squares out in different directions to create interesting patterns. You could also turn the block into a blanket pattern by chaining a multiple of 22 and repeating the pattern as needed.

Pattern

Foundation row: With colour A, ch22 + 1 turning ch.

Working from chart: Start at the bottom right-hand corner of the chart and work in double crochet, beginning the first row in the 2nd ch from hook. Each square represents 1 stitch. Right-side rows are read from right to left and wrong-side rows are read from left to right. Remember to ch1 at the beginning of each row for a turning ch (this does not count as a stitch).

To change to a different colour in the middle of a row: Work to 1 stitch before the colour change. Begin this stitch normally, working to the last yarn over, then drop the current colour to the wrong side of the work, pick up the new colour and use it to complete the stitch.

To change to a different colour at the beginning of a row: Work the last stitch of the last row as for colour changes in the middle of the row, then turn and ch1 with the new colour.

Chart

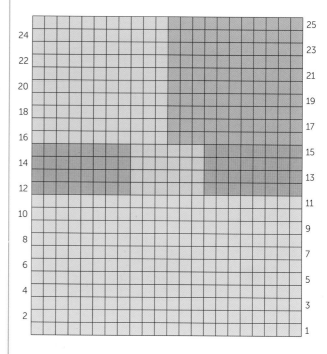

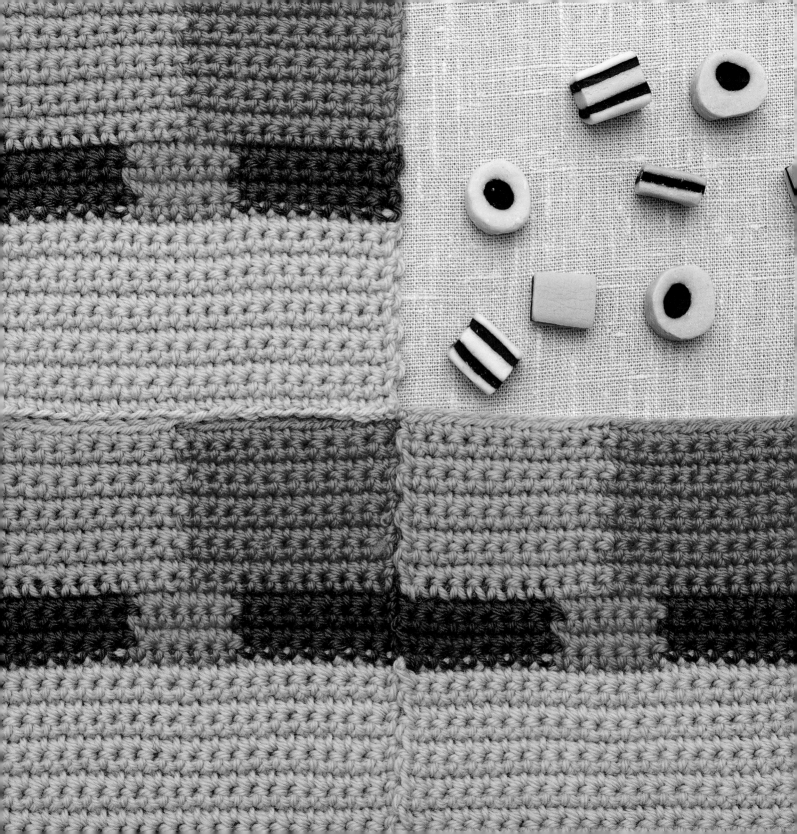

- **Hook:** 5mm
- **Yarn:** DK; quantities below are per block (see also page 124)
- **Tension:** Each block = 15cm (6in) square
- **Reversible**

A: 2m (2.2yd)

B: 2.5m (2.8yd)

C: 3.5m (3.9yd)

D: 4.5m (5yd)

E: 5.5m (6.1yd)

F: 9m (9.9yd)

G: 11m (12.1yd)

KEY

o   ch

·   sl st

+   dc

◄   begin row or round

Log Cabin

Inspired by quilt designs, this block is a great way to use up scraps just like quilters do. You can lay the squares out in different ways to create colour patterns.

Pattern

Foundation row: With colour A, ch6.

Row 1: Beg in 2nd ch from hook, dc in next 5ch, turn. (5 sts)

Row 2: Ch1, dc in each st to end, turn.

Rows 3–5: Repeat row 2, changing to colour B on last st of row 5. End colour A.

Row 6: Ch1, turn work 90 degrees clockwise, dc in next 4 row ends, 3dc in first foundation ch, dc in next 4 foundation ch, turn. (11 sts)

Row 7: Ch1, dc in 5 sts, 3dc in next st, dc in 5 sts, turn. (13 sts)

Row 8: Ch1, dc in 6 sts, 3dc in next st, dc in 6 sts, changing to colour C on last st. End colour B. (15 sts)

Row 9: Ch1, turn work 90 degrees clockwise, dc in first 7 row ends, 3dc in next st, dc in next 4 sts and next 3 row ends, turn. (17 sts)

Row 10: Ch1, dc in 8 sts, 3dc in next st, dc in 8 sts, turn. (19 sts)

Row 11: Ch1, dc in 9 sts, 3dc in next st, dc in 9 sts, changing to colour D on last st. End colour C. (21 sts)

Row 12: Ch1, turn work 90 degrees clockwise, dc in next 3 row ends and next 7 sts, 3dc in next st, dc in next 7 sts and next 3 row ends, turn. (23 sts)

Row 13: Ch1, dc in 11 sts, 3dc in next st, dc in 11 sts, turn. (25 sts)

Row 14: Ch1, dc in 12 sts, 3dc in next st, dc in 12 sts, changing to colour E on last st. End colour D. (27 sts)

Row 15: Ch1, turn work 90 degrees clockwise, dc in next 3 row ends and next 10 sts, 3dc in next st, dc in next 10 sts and next 3 row ends, turn. (29 sts)

Chart

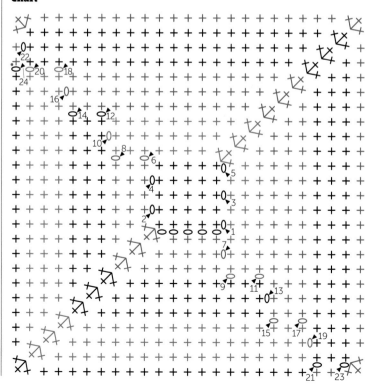

Row 16: Ch1, dc in 14 sts, 3dc in next st, dc in 14 sts, turn. (31 sts)

Row 17: Ch1, dc in 15 sts, 3dc in next st, dc in 15 sts, changing to colour F on last st. End colour E. (33 sts)

Row 18: Ch1, turn work 90 degrees clockwise, dc in next 3 row ends and next 13 sts, 3dc in next st, dc in next 13 sts and next 3 row ends, turn. (35 sts)

Row 19: Ch1, dc in 17 sts, 3dc in next st, dc in 17 sts, turn. (37 sts)

Row 20: Ch1, dc in 18 sts, 3dc in next st, dc in 18 sts, changing to colour G on last st. End colour F. (39 sts)

Row 21: Ch1, turn work 90 degrees clockwise, dc in next 3 row ends and next 16 sts, 3dc in next st, dc in next 16 sts and next 3 row ends, turn. (41 sts)

Row 22: Ch1, dc in 20 sts, 3dc in next st, dc in 20 sts, turn. (43 sts)

Row 23: Ch1, dc in 21 sts, 3dc in next st, dc in 21 sts. End colour G. (45 sts)

Rnd 24 (edging): Turn work 90 degrees clockwise and join colour F in first st worked in colour F, ch1 and dc in same st, dc in next 18 sts, 3dc in next st, dc in next 19 sts, changing to colour G on last st. Continue with colour G, dc in next 2 row ends, 3dc in next st, [dc in next 21 sts, 3dc in next st] twice, dc in next 2 row ends, sl st in first dc made. End both colours. (96 sts)

Skill level: 2

- **Hook:** 5mm
- **Yarn:** DK; quantities below are for afghan shown (see also page 124)
- **Tension:** 12 sts and 7 rows = 10cm (4in) square
- **Afghan size:** 150 x 175cm (60 x 70in) including edging

A: 196m (215yd)

B: 300m (329yd)

C: 280m (307yd)

D: 196m (215yd)

E: 196m (215yd)

F: 196m (215yd)

G: 196m (215yd)

H: 196m (215yd)

I: 196m (215yd)

J: 196m (215yd)

K: 196m (215yd)

L: 196m (215yd)

Holi Festival Blanket

This afghan is made with a big palette of bright colours inspired by the spice-throwing Indian festival, Holi. Rows of treble crochet, granny stripes and V-stitches make up the deceptively simple design. The only stitches used are actually treble crochet and chain stitches. All rows are worked from the right side so there is no turning involved, which is great as the blanket grows in size.

Turn the page for the chart and pattern instructions.

KEY

○ ch

T tr

◄ begin row or round

Pattern

Foundation row: With colour A, loosely ch a multiple of 3 + 2 + 3 turning ch. To match afghan shown, ch179.

Row 1: Beg in 5th ch from hook, (first ch3 counts as 1 tr), tr in each ch to end. End colour A.

Row 2: Join colour B in first st of last row, ch3 (counts as 1 tr), tr in each st to end. End colour B.

Row 3: Repeat row 2 using colour C.

Row 4: Join colour D in first st of last row, ch3 (counts as 1 tr), [skip 1 st, 3tr in next st, skip 1 st] to last st, tr in last st. End colour D.

Row 5: Join colour E in first st of last row, ch3 (counts as 1 tr), tr in same place, [skip 3 sts, 3tr in gap before next st] to last 4 sts, skip 3 sts, 2tr in last st. End colour E.

Row 6: Join colour F in first st of last row, ch3 (counts as 1 tr), skip 1 st, [3tr in gap before next st, skip 3 sts] to last 2 sts, 3tr in gap before next st, skip 1 st, tr in last st. End colour F.

Row 7: Repeat row 5 using colour G.

Row 8: Repeat row 6 using colour H.

Row 9: Join colour I in first st of last row, ch3 (counts as 1 tr), tr in each st to end. End colour I.

Row 10: Join colour J in first st of last row, ch3 (counts as 1 tr), [skip 1 st, V-st in next st, skip 1 st] to last st, tr in last st. End colour J.

Row 11: Join colour K in first st of last row, ch3 (counts as 1 tr),

[skip 1 st, V-st in ch1sp, skip 1 st] to last st, tr in last st. End colour K.

Row 12: Repeat row 11 using colour L.

Row 13: Join colour A in first st of last row, ch3 (counts as 1 tr), [skip 1 st, 3tr in ch1sp, skip 1 st] to last st, tr in last st. End colour A.

Row 14: Repeat row 9 using colour B.

Repeat rows 2–14 until fabric is the desired length, changing to the next colour in the established sequence (A–L) on each row. To match afghan shown, work 58 repeats across and work the row repeat 9 times in total (118 rows).

Next 2 rows: Repeat row 2 twice, using next two colours in sequence (K and L to match afghan shown).

Edging

Rnd 1: Join colour C in top-right corner st, ch1, (dc, htr, dc) in corner st, dc in each st to last st of edge, (dc, htr, dc) in last st, [dc around post of tr, dc in base of same tr] in each row end along side, (dc, htr, dc) in first foundation ch, dc in each ch to last ch, (dc, htr, dc) in last ch, [dc around post of tr, dc in top of same tr] in each row end along side, sl st in first dc made. End colour C.

Rnd 2: Join colour B in corner htr, ch3 (counts as 1 tr), 4tr in same place, [tr in each st to next corner htr, 5tr in corner htr] 3 times, tr in each st to end, sl st in top of beg ch3. End colour B.

Chart

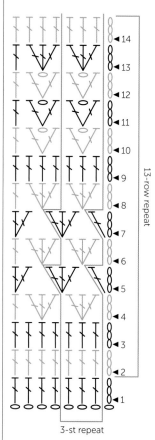

13-row repeat

3-st repeat

A simple treble crochet edging is easy to add and gives a neat finish to the blanket.

This rainbow blanket is perfect for relaxing on the sofa all year round – celebrating the summer or bringing colour and warmth to a winter evening.

SPECIAL STITCH

V-stitch (V-st):
(Tr, ch1, tr) in place indicated.

- **Hook:** 5mm

- **Yarn:** DK (see page 124 for quantities)

- **Tension:** 20 sts and approx. 6½ rows in tr = 10cm (4in) square

A

B

C

D

KEY

○ ch

┬ tr

◄ begin row

← direction of work

Neon Frills

This pattern is a simple eyelet fabric decorated with surface crochet. There are frills on alternate eyelet rows, but you could add frills on every eyelet row for a really frilly fabric. You could also omit the frills for a simple and very easy afghan. Use up all those scraps you have and experiment with different types of yarn for the frills.

Pattern

Foundation row: With colour A, ch a multiple of 2 + 1 + 3 turning ch.

Row 1 (RS): Beg in 5th ch from hook (first ch3 counts as 1 tr), tr in each ch to end, turn.

Row 2 (WS): Ch3 (counts as 1 tr), tr in next st, [ch1, skip 1 st, tr in next st] to last st, tr in last st, turn.

Row 3: Ch3 (counts as 1 tr), tr in each st and ch1sp to end, turn.

Repeat rows 2 + 3 until fabric is the desired length, ending with a row 3. End colour A.

Surface crochet frill: With RS facing, join colour B, C or D around top of post of 2nd stitch on right-hand side of row 2, ch3 (counts as 1 tr), 2tr around same post, ch1, [starting at bottom of the next st on row 2, work 3tr around post, ch1, starting at top of next st on row 2, work 3tr around post, ch1] to end of row, ending last repeat by omitting the last ch1. End colour.

Work frills on every other repeat of row 2, alternating colours as desired.

Charts

surface crochet frill

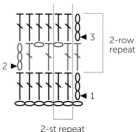

2-row repeat

2-st repeat

- **Hook:** 5mm
- **Yarn:** DK; quantities below are per block (see also page 124)
- **Tension:** Each block = 15cm (6in) square

A: 5m (5.5yd)

B: 5m (5.5yd)

C: 5m (5.5yd)

D: 5m (5.5yd)

E: 9m (9.9yd)

KEY

o   ch

•   sl st

+   dc

T   htr

T   tr

◄   begin row or round

Pastel Rows

This is a super easy block to crochet. All rows are worked from the right side, so there is no turning involved. Experiment with laying out the squares at alternating angles to create different patterns. The block is great for using up scraps from your stash, or it can be worked in shades of one colour.

Pattern

Foundation row: With colour A, ch23.

Row 1: Beg in 5th ch from hook (first ch3 counts as 1 tr), tr in each ch to end. End colour A. (20 sts)

Row 2: Join colour B in first st of last row, ch3 (counts as 1 tr), tr in each st to end. End colour B. Do not turn.

Row 3: Repeat row 2 using colour C.

Row 4: Repeat row 2 using colour D.

Row 5: Repeat row 2 using colour B.

Row 6: Repeat row 2 using colour E.

Row 7: Repeat row 2 using colour A.

Row 8: Repeat row 2 using colour C.

Row 9: Repeat row 2 using colour D.

Edging

Rnd 10: Join colour E in last st made, ch1, (dc, htr, dc) in same place, working along side of block, [2dc around post of next st] 9 times, (dc, htr, dc) in first foundation ch, dc in next 18 ch, (dc, htr, dc) in next ch, [2dc around post of next st] 9 times, (dc, htr, dc) in top of next st, dc in next 18 sts, sl st in first dc made. End colour E.

Chart

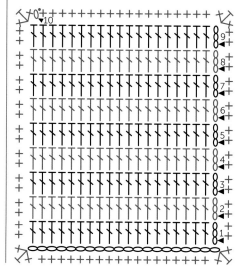

- **Hook:** 5mm
- **Yarn:** DK; quantities below are per block (see also page 124)
- **Tension:** Each block = 15cm (6in) square
- **Reversible**

A: 2m (2.2yd)

B: 4m (4.4yd)

C: 6m (6.6yd)

D: 8m (8.8yd)

E: 10m (11yd)

F: 12m (13.2yd)

KEY

o   ch

•   sl st

⊤   tr

⌇   FPtr

⌇   BPtr

◄   begin round

Reversi

Alternating sides of back post and front post stitches create a block that looks the same on both front and back. Due to the nature of post stitches, the blocks tend to be a bit unshapely when crocheted but become more square when joined up. The design has a lovely squishiness to it, creating a warm and cosy blanket.

Pattern

Foundation ring: With colour A, ch4, sl st in first ch to form a ring.

Rnd 1: Ch3 (counts as 1 tr), 2tr in ring, [ch2, 3tr in ring] 3 times, ch2, sl st in top of beg ch3. End colour A. (12 sts, 4 chsp)

Rnd 2: Join colour B in ch2sp, ch3 (counts as 1 tr), tr in same place, *BPtr in next 3 sts, (2tr, ch2, 2tr) in ch2sp, FPtr in next 3 sts**, (2tr, ch2, 2tr) in ch2sp; rep from * to ** once more, 2tr in ch2sp, ch2, sl st in top of beg ch3. End colour B. (28 sts, 4 chsp)

Rnd 3: Join colour C in ch2sp, ch3 (counts as 1 tr), tr in same place, *BPtr in next 7 sts, (2tr, ch2, 2tr) in ch2sp, FPtr in next 7 sts**, (2tr, ch2, 2tr) in ch2sp; rep from * to ** once more, 2tr in ch2sp, ch2, sl st in top of beg ch3. End colour C. (44 sts, 4 chsp)

Rnd 4: Join colour D in ch2sp, ch3 (counts as 1 tr), tr in same place, *BPtr in next 11 sts, (2tr, ch2, 2tr) in ch2sp, FPtr in next 11 sts**, (2tr, ch2, 2tr) in ch2sp; rep from * to ** once more, 2tr in ch2sp, ch2, sl st in top of beg ch3. End colour D. (60 sts, 4 chsp)

Rnd 5: Join colour E in ch2sp, ch3 (counts as 1 tr), tr in same place, *BPtr in next 15 sts, (2tr, ch2, 2tr) in ch2sp, FPtr in next 15 sts**, (2tr, ch2, 2tr) in ch2sp; rep from * to ** once more, 2tr in ch2sp, ch2, sl st in top of beg ch3. End colour E. (76 sts, 4 chsp)

Rnd 6: Join colour F in ch2sp, ch3 (counts as 1 tr), tr in same place, *BPtr in next 19 sts, (2tr, ch2, 2tr) in ch2sp, FPtr in next 19 sts**, (2tr, ch2, 2tr) in ch2sp; rep from * to ** once more, 2tr in ch2sp, ch2, sl st in top of beg ch3. End colour F. (92 sts, 4 chsp)

Sample is shown with Knitty edging (page 104).

Chart

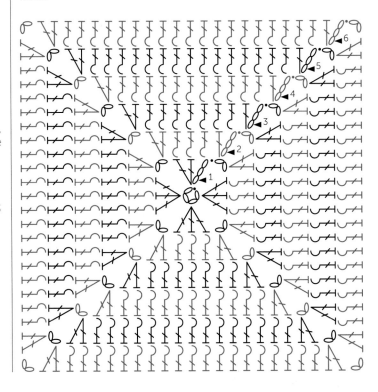

- **Hook:** 6mm
- **Yarn:** DK (see page 124 for quantities)
- **Tension:** Approx. 13½ sts and 13½ rows = 10cm (4in) square
- **Reversible**

A

B

C

D

KEY

○ ch

+ dc

⋏ dc3tog

◄ begin row

Rice Field

This pattern is easy to remember and can be worked in anything from two to many colours. The stitch pattern makes a dense fabric, so use a larger hook size than you would normally. This pattern looks great on both right and wrong sides, making it a perfect design for throws. Try working the pattern in an even larger hook size for a looser texture, or use a self-striping yarn for colour changes without the need to weave in ends.

Pattern

Foundation row: With colour A, loosely ch a multiple of 2 + 1 + 1 turning ch.

Row 1 (RS): Dc in 2nd ch from hook, [dc3tog, ch1] to last 2 ch, dc3tog, dc in last ch. End colour A. Turn.

Row 2 (WS): Join colour B, ch1, dc in first st, dc3tog, [ch1, dc3tog] to end, dc in last st. End colour B. Turn.

Row 3: Repeat row 2 using colour C.

Row 4: Repeat row 2 using colour D.

Row 5: Repeat row 2 using colour A.

Repeat rows 2–5 until fabric is the desired length.

Sample is shown with Crab edging (page 105).

Chart

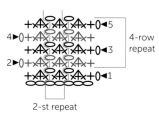

4-row repeat

2-st repeat

SPECIAL STITCH

Double crochet 3 together (dc3tog):

Insert hook in same ch or st as last st worked and draw up a loop (2 loops on hook), [insert hook in next ch or st and draw up a loop] twice (4 loops on hook), yo and pull through all 4 loops on hook.

- **Hook:** 5mm
- **Yarn:** DK (see page 124 for quantities)
- **Tension:** Approx. 13½ sts and 12½ rows = 10cm (4in) square

A

B

C

D

E

F

G

KEY

○ ch

+ dc

⊤ tr

⊥ qtr

⋏ qtr2tog

◄ begin row

Textured Ripple

This highly textured fabric looks like a crocheted ripple pattern, but is actually created by working stitches into previous rows. After rows 1–7, there are only two rows to remember. The sample uses a large colour palette, but this design would look equally splendid in a smaller palette.

Chart

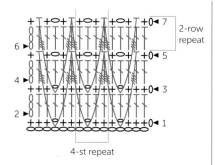

2-row repeat

4-st repeat

Pattern

Foundation row: With colour A, ch a multiple of 4 + 3 + 1 turning ch.

Row 1 (RS): Dc in 2nd ch from hook, [dc in next 2 ch, ch1, skip 1 ch, dc in next ch] to last 2 ch, dc in last 2 ch, turn.

Row 2 (WS): Ch3 (counts as 1 tr), tr in each st and ch1sp to end, turn.

Row 3: Ch1, dc in first st, [dc in next 2 sts, ch1, skip 1 st, dc in next st] to last 2 sts, dc in last 2 sts, turn.

Row 4: Repeat row 2. End colour A.

Row 5: Join colour B, ch1, dc in first st, qtr in first skipped ch of foundation row, dc in next st, ch1, skip 1 st, dc in next st, [qtr2tog in

skipped ch just worked into and next skipped ch of foundation row, dc in next st, ch1, skip 1 st, dc in next st] to last 2 sts, qtr in last skipped ch just worked into, dc in last st, turn.

Row 6: Repeat row 2. End colour B.

Row 7: Join colour C, ch1, dc in first st, qtr in first skipped st 5 rows below, dc in next st, ch1, skip 1 st, dc in next st, [qtr2tog in last skipped st just worked into and next skipped st 5 rows below, dc in next st, ch1, skip 1 st, dc in next st] to last 2 sts, qtr in last skipped st just worked into, dc in last st, turn.

Row 8: Repeat row 2. End colour C.

Repeat rows 7 + 8 for pattern, changing colour as follows:

Rows 9 + 10: Colour D.

Rows 11 + 12: Colour E.

Rows 13 + 14: Colour F.

Rows 15 + 16: Colour G.

Continue repeating rows 7 + 8 using colours A–G in established sequence until fabric is the desired length. End with a row 7.

SPECIAL STITCHES

Quadruple treble (qtr):
[Yo] 4 times, insert hook in place indicated and draw up a loop (6 loops on hook), [yo and pull through 2 loops] 5 times (1 loop remains on hook).

Quadruple treble 2 together (qtr2tog):
[Yo] 4 times, insert hook in previous skipped st 5 rows below and draw up a loop (6 loops on hook), [yo and pull through 2 loops] 4 times (2 loops on hook), [yo] 4 times, insert hook in next skipped st 5 rows below and draw up a loop (7 loops on hook), [yo and pull through 2 loops] 4 times, yo and pull through remaining 3 loops on hook.

- **Hook:** 6mm

- **Yarn:** DK (see page 124 for quantities)

- **Tension:** 12½ sts and 8½ rows = 10cm (4in) square

- **Reversible**

A

B

C

D

E

F

G

KEY

○ ch

+ dc

‡ Ext dc

⦵ beg PS

○ PS

◄ begin row

Carnival

Pineapple stitches gives this pattern a lovely, spongy feel. A rainbow palette works great for this design – the more colours, the better. The first and last rows use extended double crochet to straighten out the edges.

Pattern

Foundation row: With colour A, ch a multiple of 10 + 5 + 1 turning ch.

Row 1: Beg in 2nd ch from hook, [Ext dc in next 5 ch, PS in next 5 ch] to last 5 ch, Ext dc in last 5 ch. End colour A. Turn.

Row 2: Join colour B, beg PS in first st, PS in next 4 sts, [dc in next 5 PS, PS in next 5 sts] to end. End colour B. Turn.

Row 3: Join colour C, ch1, [dc in first 5 sts, PS in next 5 sts] to last 5 sts, dc in last 5 sts. End colour C. Turn.

Repeat rows 2 + 3 in the following colour sequence, working 1 row of each colour: colour D, colour E, colour F, colour G.

Continue repeating rows 2 + 3 using colours A–G in established sequence until fabric is the desired length. End with a row 2.

SPECIAL STITCHES

Extended double crochet (Ext dc):

Insert hook in place indicated and draw up a loop (2 loops on hook), ch1, yo and pull through both loops on hook.

Beginning pineapple stitch (beg PS):

Ch2, yo, insert hook in place indicated and draw up a loop (3 loops on hook), [yo and pull through 2 loops on hook] twice.

Pineapple stitch (PS):

[Yo, insert hook in place indicated and draw up a loop] twice (5 loops on hook), yo and pull through 4 loops on hook, yo and pull through remaining 2 loops on hook.

Chart

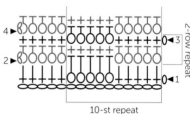

2-row repeat

10-st repeat

- **Hook:** 6mm
- **Yarn:** DK (see page 124 for quantities)
- **Tension:** Approx. 13½ sts and 16 rows = 10cm (4in) square
- **Crochet technique:** Intarsia (page 119)
- **Reversible**

A

B

Checkmate

This simple chequerboard pattern looks great from both sides. You could work the design in more than two colours. Try winding the necessary amount of yarn to work each square on to bobbins or pegs to help stop the yarn from tangling.

Pattern

Foundation row: With colour A, ch a multiple of 20 + 1 turning ch.

Working from chart: Start at the bottom right-hand corner of the chart and work in double crochet, beginning the first row in the 2nd ch from hook. Each square represents 1 stitch. Right-side rows are read from right to left and wrong-side rows are read from left to right. Remember to ch1 at the beginning of each row for a turning ch (this does not count as a stitch).

To change to a different colour in the middle of a row: Work to 1 stitch before the colour change. Begin this stitch normally, working to the last yarn over, then drop the current colour to the wrong side of the work, pick up the new colour and use it to complete the stitch.

To change to a different colour at the beginning of a row: Work the last stitch of the last row as for colour changes in the middle of the row, then turn and ch1 with the new colour.

Chart

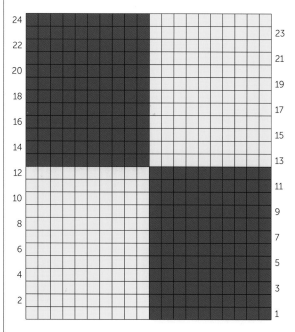

- **Hook:** 5mm
- **Yarn:** DK; quantities below are per block (see also page 124)
- **Tension:** Each block = 15cm (6in) square
- **Afghan size:** 90cm (36in) square; 36 blocks joined in 6 rows of 6 blocks

A: 3.5m (3.9yd)

B: 17m (18.6yd)

C: 16m (17.5yd)

D: 3.5m (3.9yd)

Diagonals Baby Blanket

This easy pattern provides lots of opportunities for experimenting with colour and layout. The stitches are close fitting, so it is a perfect design for babies. The pattern would also look great worked in greyscale for a geometric throw.

Turn the page for the chart and pattern instructions.

KEY

- ○ ch
- • sl st
- + dc
- ⋋⫝̸ dc2tog
- ⋋⫝̸⋋ dc3tog
- ◄ begin row or round

Pattern

Foundation row: With colour A, ch2.

Row 1: 3dc in 2nd ch from hook, turn. (3 sts)

Row 2: Ch1, 2dc in first st, dc in next st, 2dc in last st, turn. (5 sts)

Row 3: Ch1, 2dc in first st, dc in each st to last st, 2dc in last st, turn. (7 sts)

Rows 4 + 5: Repeat row 3. (11 sts)

Row 6: Ch1, dc in each st to end, turn.

Rows 7 + 8: Repeat row 3. End colour A. (15 sts)

Row 9: Join colour B and repeat row 3. (17 sts)

Row 10: Repeat row 6.

Rows 11 + 12: Repeat row 3. End colour B. Turn. (21 sts)

Row 13: Join colour C and repeat row 3. (23 sts)

Row 14: Repeat row 6.

Rows 15–17: Repeat row 3. (29 sts)

Row 18: Repeat row 6. End colour C.

Row 19: Join colour B and repeat row 3. (31 sts)

Row 20: Ch1, dc2tog, dc in each st to last 2 sts, dc2tog. End colour B. Turn. (29 sts)

Row 21: Join colour C and repeat row 6.

Rows 22–24: Repeat row 20. (23 sts)

Row 25: Repeat row 6.

Row 26: Repeat row 20. End colour C. Turn. (21 sts)

Rows 27 + 28: Join colour B and repeat row 20. (17 sts)

Row 29: Repeat row 6.

Row 30: Repeat row 20. End colour B. Turn. (15 sts)

Rows 31 + 32: Join colour D and repeat row 20. (11 sts)

Row 33: Repeat row 6.

Rows 34–37: Repeat row 20. (3 sts)

Row 38: Ch1, dc3tog. End colour D. (1 st)

Rnd 39 (edging): Turn block over and join colour B in any corner, ch1, *(dc, htr, dc) in corner, dc in each of next 19 row ends to next corner; rep from * 3 times more, sl st in first dc made. End colour B. (88 sts)

To make baby blanket: Make 36 blocks. Using colour B, join the blocks with a crochet seam, matching the colours at the corners to create a diamond pattern. Add Crab edging (page 105).

Chart

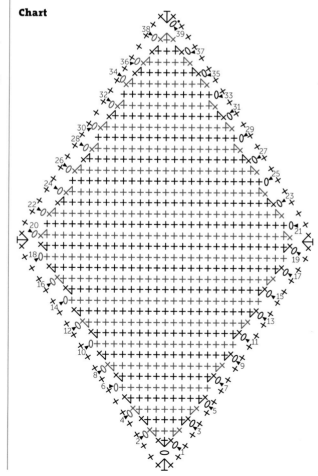

SPECIAL STITCHES

Double crochet 2 together (dc2tog):

Work dc in each of next 2 sts but omit final yo of each dc, yo and pull through all 3 loops on hook.

Double crochet 3 together (dc3tog):

Work dc in each of next 3 sts but omit final yo of each dc, yo and pull through all 4 loops on hook.

This blanket is finished with a simple crab stitch edging, but alternatively you could use Mosaic edging (page 106) for a fuller border, incorporating all the project colours.

- **Hook:** 5mm
- **Yarn:** DK (see page 124 for quantities)
- **Tension:** 12 sts and 14 rows = 10cm (4in) wide x 15cm (6in) high

A

B

C

D

E

KEY

○ ch

+ dc

⊥ Ext dc

ᔐ dc in place indicated

┬ tr

◄ begin row

Coral Shells

This design and colour palette is reminiscent of summer holidays at the seaside. Try working in cotton or linen yarn for a beach throw.

Pattern

Foundation row: With colour A, ch a multiple of 6 + 5 + 1 turning ch.

Row 1 (RS): Beg in 2nd ch from hook, Ext dc in each ch to end. End colour A. Turn.

Row 2 (WS): Join colour B, ch1, Ext dc in each st to end. End colour B. Turn.

Row 3: Repeat row 2 using colour C.

Row 4: Repeat row 2 using colour D.

Row 5: Repeat row 2 using colour E.

Row 6: Repeat row 2 using colour A.

Row 7: Join colour B, ch1, dc in first 3 sts, [skip 2 sts, Shell in next st, skip 2 sts, dc in next st] to last 8 sts, skip 2 sts, Shell in next st, skip 2 sts, dc in last 3 sts. End colour B. Turn.

Row 8: Join colour C, ch3 (counts as 1 tr), tr in next 2 sts, ch5, skip Shell, [(tr, ch1, tr) in next dc, ch5, skip Shell] to last 3 sts, tr in last 3 sts, turn.

Row 9: Ch3 (counts as 1 tr), tr in next st, 4tr in next st, dc in 4th tr of Shell 2 rows below, working over

ch5sp of previous row, [skip 1 st, Shell in ch1sp, skip 1 st, dc in 4th tr of Shell 2 rows below, working over ch5sp of previous row] to last 3 sts, 4tr in next st, tr in last 2 sts. End colour C. Turn.

Row 10: Join colour D, ch1, dc in first 3 sts, ch2, skip 3 sts, [(tr, ch1, tr) in dc, ch5, skip Shell] to last 7 sts, (tr, ch1, tr) in dc, ch2, skip 3 sts, dc in last 3 sts, turn.

Row 11: Ch1, 1 dc in first 3 sts, [skip 1 st, Shell in ch1sp, dc in 4th tr of Shell 2 rows below, working over ch5sp of previous row] to last 5 sts, skip 1 st, Shell in ch1sp, skip 1 st, dc in last 3 sts. End colour D. Turn.

Row 12: Join colour E, ch3 (counts as 1 tr), tr in next 2 sts, ch5, skip Shell, [(tr, ch1, tr) in next dc, ch5, skip Shell] to last 3 sts, tr in last 3 sts, turn.

Row 13: Ch3 (counts as 1 tr), tr in next st, 4tr in next st, [dc in 4th tr of Shell 2 rows below, working over ch5sp of previous row, skip 1 st, Shell in ch1sp, skip 1 st] to last ch5sp, dc in 4th tr of Shell 2 rows below, working over ch5sp of previous row, 4tr in next st, tr in last 2 sts. End colour E. Turn.

Row 14: Join colour A, ch1, dc in first 3 sts, ch2, skip 3 sts, tr in dc, [ch2, skip 3 sts, dc in 4th tr of Shell,

ch2, skip 3 sts, tr in dc] to last 6 sts, ch2, skip 3 sts, dc in last 3 sts, turn.

Row 15: Ch1, Ext dc in first 3 sts, 2Ext dc in ch2sp, [Ext dc in tr, 2Ext dc in ch2sp, Ext dc in dc, 2Ext dc in ch2sp] to last 4 sts and ch2sp, Ext dc in next tr, 2Ext dc in ch2sp, Ext dc in last 3 sts. End colour A. Turn.

Repeat rows 2–15 until fabric is the desired length, ending with a row 6.

Chart

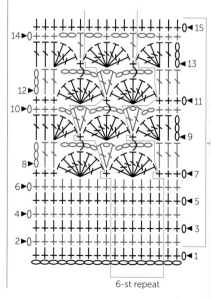

6-st repeat

SPECIAL STITCHES

Extended double crochet (Ext dc):
Insert hook in place indicated and draw up a loop (2 loops on hook), ch1, yo and pull through both loops on hook.

Shell:
Work 7tr in place indicated.

- **Hook:** 5mm
- **Yarn:** DK; quantities below are per block (see also page 124)
- **Tension:** Each block = 15cm (6in) square

A: 14.5m (15.9yd)

B: 15.5m (17yd)

KEY

o   ch

•   sl st

+   dc

ƚ   BPdc

T   htr

ƒ   tr

◄   begin round

Strawberries and Cream

This square begins in the same way as a traditional granny square, but is edged with a shell border. The sample is worked in two colours, but it would look just as good in multiple colours. Try working the first three rounds in bright colours, then work the last four rounds in neutrals.

Pattern

Foundation ring: With colour A, ch4, sl st in first ch to form a ring.

Rnd 1: Ch3 (counts as 1 tr), 2tr in ring, [ch2, 3tr in ring] 3 times, ch2, sl st in top of beg ch3. End colour A. (12 sts, 4 chsp)

Rnd 2: Join colour B in next ch2sp, ch3 (counts as 1 tr), (2tr, ch2, 3tr) in same place, *ch1, (3tr, ch2, 3tr) in ch2sp; rep from * twice more, ch1, sl st in top of beg ch3. End colour B. (24 sts, 8 chsp)

Rnd 3: Join colour A in next ch2sp, ch3 (counts as 1 tr), (2tr, ch2, 3tr) in same place, *ch1, 3tr in ch1sp, ch1, (3tr, ch2, 3tr) in ch2sp; rep from * twice more, ch1, 3tr in ch1sp, ch1, sl st in top of beg ch3. End colour A. (36 sts, 12 chsp)

Rnd 4: Join colour B in next ch2sp, ch1, *(dc, ch3, dc) in ch2sp, [dc in next 3 sts, dc in ch1sp] twice, dc in next 3 sts; rep from * 3 times more, sl st in first dc made. End colour B. (52 sts, 4 chsp)

Rnd 5: Join colour A in next ch3sp, ch3 (counts as 1 tr), 6tr in same place, *skip 2 sts, [dc in next st, skip 1 st, 5tr in next st, skip 1 st] twice, dc in next st, skip 2 sts**, 7tr in ch3sp; rep from * twice more, then from * to ** once,

sl st in top of beg ch3. End colour A. (80 sts)

Rnd 6: Join colour B in 4th tr of corner shell, ch1, *(dc, ch2, dc) in 4th tr of corner shell, ch3, skip 3 sts, [tr in next dc, ch2, BPdc in 3rd tr of 5tr group, ch2, skip 2 sts] twice, tr in next dc, ch3, skip 3 sts; rep from * 3 times

more, sl st in first dc made. (28 sts, 28 chsp)

Rnd 7: Sl st in corner ch2sp, ch1, *(dc, htr, dc) in ch2sp, dc in next st, 3dc in ch3sp, [dc in next st, 2dc in ch2sp] 4 times, dc in next st, 3dc in ch3sp, dc in next st; rep from * 3 times more, sl st in first dc made. End colour B. (96 sts)

Chart

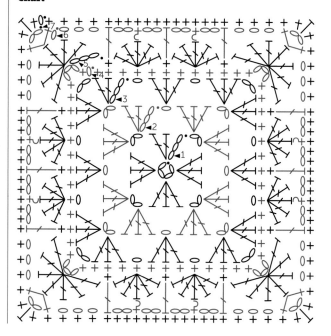

- **Hook:** 5mm
- **Yarn:** DK; quantities below are per block (see also page 124)
- **Tension:** Each block = 15cm (6in) square

A: 5m (5.5yd)

B: 7m (7.7yd)

C: 9.5m (10.4yd)

D: 7m (7.7yd)

KEY

○ ch

• sl st

+ dc

T htr

† tr

‡ dtr

beg CL

CL

◄ begin round

Fizzy Mint

A fresh, zingy palette makes this block great for summer afghans. It could be worked in cotton or linen yarn for a summer picnic blanket, or try using warm wools and earthy shades for a cosy fireside throw.

Pattern

Foundation ring: With colour A, ch5, sl st in first ch to form a ring.

Rnd 1: Beg CL in ring, [ch2, CL in ring] 5 times, ch2, sl st in top of beg CL. End colour A. (6 CL, 6 chsp)

Rnd 2: Join colour B in ch2sp, ch3 (counts as 1 tr), (tr, ch1, 2tr) in same place, *ch1, (2tr, ch1, 2tr) in next ch2sp; rep from * 4 times more, ch1, sl st in top of beg ch3. End colour B. (24 sts, 12 chsp)

Rnd 3: Join colour C in next ch1sp, ch1 and dc in same place, [ch2, skip 2 sts, dc in ch1sp] 11 times, ch2, sl st in first dc made. End colour C. (12 sts, 12 chsp)

Rnd 4: Join colour A in next ch2sp, ch1, [3dc in ch2sp, ch1, skip 1 st] 11 times, 3dc in next ch2sp, ch1, skip 1 st, sl st in first dc made. End colour A. (36 sts, 12 chsp)

Rnd 5: Join colour C in previous ch1sp, ch1 and dc in same place, [ch3, skip 3 sts, dc in ch1sp] 11 times, ch3, skip 3 sts, sl st in first dc made. End colour C. (12 sts, 12 chsp)

Rnd 6: Join colour D in next ch3sp, ch3 (counts as 1 tr), 2tr in same place, ch1, *skip 1 st, (3dtr, ch2, 3dtr) in ch3sp**, [ch1, skip 1 st, 3tr in ch3sp] twice, ch1; rep from * twice more, then from * to ** once, ch1, skip 1 st, 3tr in ch3sp,

ch1, sl st in top of beg ch3. End colour D. (48 sts, 16 chsp)

Rnd 7: Join colour C in ch2sp, ch1, *(dc, ch3, dc) in ch2sp, [ch3, skip 3 sts, dc in ch1sp] 3 times, ch3, skip 3 sts; rep from * 3 times more, sl st in first dc made. End colour C. (20 sts, 20 chsp)

Rnd 8: Join colour B in corner ch3sp, ch1, *(dc, htr, dc) in ch3sp, [ch1, skip 1 st, 3dc in ch3sp]

4 times, ch1; rep from * 3 times more, sl st in first dc made. End colour B. (60 sts, 20 chsp)

Rnd 9: Join colour C, ch1, dc in first st, [3dc in htr, dc in each st and ch1sp to next htr] 3 times, 3dc in htr, dc in each st and ch1sp to end, sl st in first dc made. End colour C. (88 sts)

Sample is shown with Fancy edging (page 106).

Chart

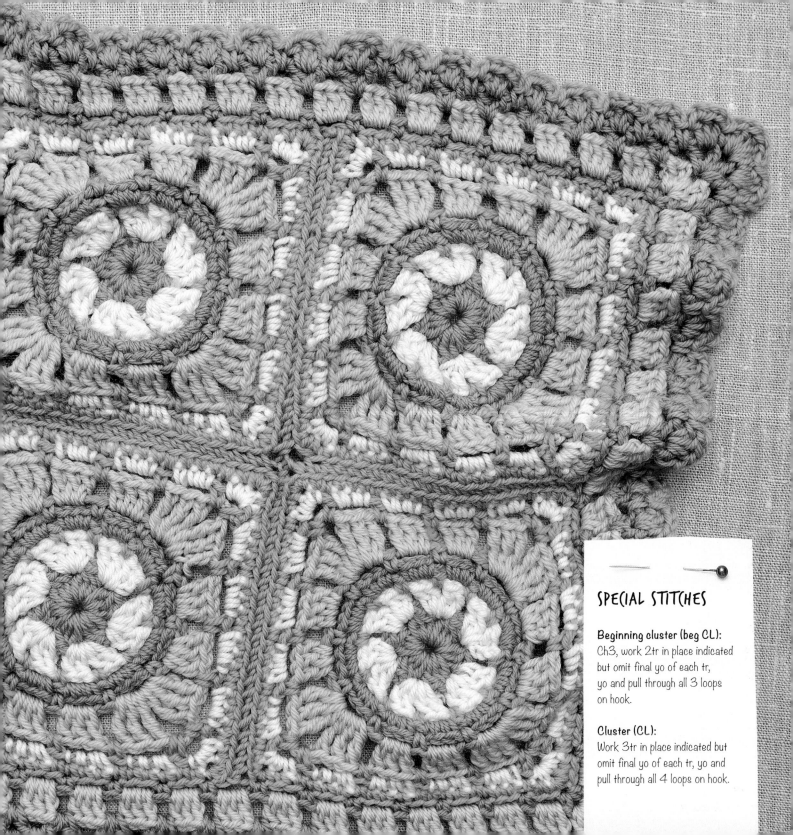

SPECIAL STITCHES

Beginning cluster (beg CL):
Ch3, work 2tr in place indicated
but omit final yo of each tr,
yo and pull through all 3 loops
on hook.

Cluster (CL):
Work 3tr in place indicated but
omit final yo of each tr, yo and
pull through all 4 loops on hook.

- **Hook:** 5mm
- **Yarn:** DK (see page 124 for quantities)
- **Tension:** 12 sts and 8½ rows = 10cm (4in) square
- **Reversible**

A

B

C

D

E

KEY

o ch

T tr

◄ begin row

Granny Stripes

Everyone loves a granny stripe blanket. The sample uses a set colour layout, but you could work the pattern in random colours for a 'homely' throw.

Pattern

Foundation row: With colour A, ch a multiple of 3 + 2 + 3 turning ch.

Row 1: Beg in 6th ch from hook (first ch3 counts as 1 tr), [3tr in next ch, skip 2 ch] to last 3 ch, 3tr in next ch, skip 1 ch, tr in last ch, turn.

Row 2: Ch3 (counts as 1 tr), tr in same place, skip 3tr, [3tr in gap before next st, skip 3tr] to last st, 2tr in last st. End colour A. Turn.

Row 3: Join colour B, ch3 (counts as 1 tr), skip 1 st, [3tr in gap before next st, skip 3 sts] to last 2 sts, 3tr in gap before next st, skip 1 st, tr in last st, turn.

Row 4: Ch3 (counts as 1 tr), tr in same place, skip 3 sts, [3tr in gap before next st, skip 3 sts] to last st, 2tr in last st. End colour B. Turn.

Rows 5 + 6: Repeat rows 3 + 4 using colour C.

Rows 7 + 8: Repeat rows 3 + 4 using colour D.

Row 9: Repeat row 3 using colour E.

Rows 10 + 11: Repeat row 4 and then row 3 using colour D.

Rows 12 + 13: Repeat row 4 and then row 3 using colour C.

Rows 14 + 15: Repeat row 4 and then row 3 using colour B.

Rows 16–18: Repeat row 4, then row 3 and then row 4 again using colour A.

Repeat rows 3–18 until fabric is the desired length.

Chart

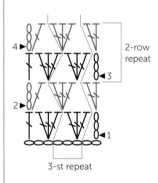

2-row repeat

3-st repeat

Skill level: **2**

- **Hook:** 5mm
- **Yarn:** DK; quantities below are per block (see also page 124)
- **Tension:** Each block = 15cm (6in) square

A: 1.5m (1.7yd)

B: 4m (4.4yd)

C: 3.5m (3.9yd)

D: 5.5m (6.1yd)

E: 6.5m (7.2yd)

F: 4.5m (5yd)

KEY

○	ch	beg CL	
•	sl st		
+	dc	CL	
T	htr	W-st	
⊤	tr	◄ begin round	
‡	dtr		

Lily Pad

The waistcoat stitches on rounds 5 and 6 create the look of knitted stitches, but you could replace these with normal double crochet stitches if you prefer. Join squares together by sewing through the double crochet stitches only, leaving the chain spaces unattached to create an interesting pattern.

Pattern

Foundation ring: With colour A, ch4, sl st in first ch to form a ring.

Rnd 1: Ch3 (counts as 1 tr), 11tr in ring, sl st in top of beg ch3. End colour A. (12 sts)

Rnd 2: Join colour B, beg CL in same place, [ch2, CL in next st] 11 times, ch2, sl st in top of beg CL. End colour B. (12 CL, 12 chsp)

Rnd 3: Join colour C in ch2sp, ch1, *2dc in ch2sp, ch1, skip CL, 2dc in next ch2sp, skip CL, (2htr, ch2, 2htr) in next ch2sp, skip CL; rep from * 3 times more, sl st in first dc made. End colour C. (32 sts, 8 chsp)

Rnd 4: Join colour D in previous ch2sp, ch3 (counts as 1 tr), (tr, dtr, 2tr) in same place, *tr in next 2 sts, ch3, skip 2 sts, dc in ch1sp, ch3, skip 2 sts, tr in next 2 sts**, (2tr, dtr, 2tr) in ch2sp; rep from * twice more, then from * to ** once, sl st in top of beg ch3. End colour D. (40 sts, 8 chsp)

Rnd 5: Join colour E in next dtr, ch3 (counts as 1 tr), (tr, dtr, 2tr) in same place, *tr in next 4 sts, ch3, W-st in next st, ch3, tr in next 4 sts**, (2tr, dtr, 2tr) in dtr; rep from * twice more, then

from * to ** once, sl st in top of beg ch3. End colour E. (56 sts, 8 chsp)

Rnd 6: Join colour F in next dtr, ch1, *(dc, htr, dc) in dtr, dc in next 6 sts, ch3, W-st in next st, ch3, dc in next 6 sts; rep from * 3 times more, sl st in first dc made. End colour F. (64 sts, 8 chsp)

Chart

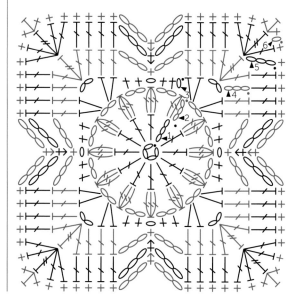

SPECIAL STITCHES

Beginning cluster (beg CL):
Ch3, work 2tr in place indicated but omit final yo of each tr, yo, pull through all 3 loops on hook.

Cluster (CL):
Work 3tr in place indicated but omit final yo of each tr, yo and pull through all 4 loops on hook.

Waistcoat stitch (W-st):
Insert hook between vertical V-shaped strands at front of indicated st and work dc.

- **Hook:** 5mm
- **Yarn:** DK; quantities below are per block (see also page 124)
- **Tension:** Each block = 15cm (6in) square

A: 9m (9.9yd)

B: 2.5m (2.8yd)

C: 4.5m (5yd)

D: 6m (6.6yd)

E: 7.5m (8.3yd)

KEY

o   ch

•   sl st

+   dc

T   htr

◄   begin round

Luxor

This simple block is quick and easy to make. Try working the half treble crochet rounds in colours to match your decor, and the double crochet rounds in a neutral colour. Staggering where new colours are joined keeps this block from twisting out of shape, which is also a good tip for traditional granny squares.

Chart

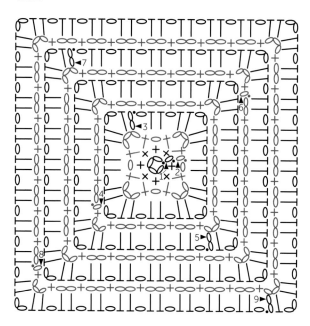

Pattern

Foundation ring: With colour A, ch4, sl st in first ch to form a ring.

Rnd 1: Ch1, 8dc in ring, sl st in first dc made. (8 sts)

Rnd 2: Ch1, (dc, ch3, dc) in same place, *ch1, skip 1 st, (dc, ch3, dc) in next st; rep from * twice more, ch1, skip 1 st, sl st in first dc made. End colour A. (8 sts, 4 chsp)

Rnd 3: Join colour B in next ch3sp, ch2 (counts as 1 htr), (htr, ch2, 2htr) in same place, *ch1, 2htr in ch1sp, ch1, (2htr, ch2, 2htr) in ch3sp; rep from * twice more, ch1, 2htr in ch1sp, ch1, sl st in top of beg ch2. End colour B. (24 sts, 12 chsp)

Rnd 4: Join colour A in next ch2sp, ch1, *(dc, ch3, dc) in ch2sp, [ch2, skip 2 sts, dc in ch1sp] twice, ch2; rep from * 3 times more, sl st in first dc made. End colour A. (16 sts, 16 chsp)

Rnd 5: Join colour C in next ch3sp, ch2 (counts as 1 htr), (htr, ch2, 2htr) in same place, *[ch1, 2htr in next ch2sp] 3 times, ch1**, (2htr, ch2, 2htr) in ch3sp; rep from * twice more, then from * to ** once, sl st in top of beg ch2. End colour C. (40 sts, 20 chsp)

Rnd 6: Join colour A in next ch2sp, ch1, *(dc, ch3, dc) in ch2sp, [ch2, skip 2 sts, dc in next ch1sp] 4 times, ch2; rep from * 3 times more, sl st in first dc made. End colour A. (24 sts, 24 chsp)

Rnd 7: Join colour D in next ch3sp, ch2 (counts as 1 htr), (htr, ch2, 2htr) in same place, *[ch1, 2htr in next ch2sp] 5 times, ch1**, (2htr, ch2, 2htr) in ch3sp; rep from * twice more, then from * to ** once, sl st in top of beg ch2. End colour D. (56 sts, 28 chsp)

Rnd 8: Join colour A in next ch2sp, ch1, *(dc, ch3, dc) in ch2sp, [ch2, skip 2 sts, dc in next ch1sp] 6 times, ch2; rep from * 3 times more, sl st in first dc made. End colour A. (32 sts, 32 chsp)

Rnd 9: Join colour E in next ch3sp, ch2 (counts as 1 htr), (htr, ch2, 2htr) in same place, *[ch1, 2htr in next ch2sp] 7 times, ch1**, (2htr, ch2, 2htr) in ch3sp; rep from * twice more, then from * to ** once, sl st in top of beg ch2. End colour E. (72 sts, 36 chsp)

- **Hook:** 5mm
- **Yarn:** DK; quantities below are per block (see also page 124)
- **Tension:** Each block = 15cm (6in) square

A: 1.5m (1.7yd)

B: 2.5m (2.8yd)

C: 4m (4.4yd)

D: 6m (6.6yd)

E: 12.5m (13.7yd)

KEY

○ ch

• sl st

+ dc

╀ tr

╪ dtr

◀ begin round

Phoenix

Phoenix is a very easy 'circle in a square' pattern. For a colourful afghan, try making the square using random, bright colours for the first three rounds and set colours for the last three rounds.

Pattern

Foundation ring: With colour A, ch4, sl st in first ch to form a ring.

Rnd 1: Ch3 (counts as 1 tr), 11tr in ring, sl st in top of beg ch3. End colour A. (12 sts)

Rnd 2: Join colour B, ch3 (counts as 1 tr), 2tr in same place, [ch1, skip 1 st, 3tr in next st] 5 times, ch1, sl st in top of beg ch3. End colour B. (18 sts, 6 chsp)

Rnd 3: Join colour C in next ch1sp, ch3 (counts as 1 tr), 2tr in same place, [skip 1 st, 3tr in next st, skip 1 st, 3tr in next ch1sp] 5 times, skip 1 st, 3tr in next st, sl st in top of beg ch3. End colour C. (36 sts)

Rnd 4: Join colour D in next st, ch3 (counts as 1 tr), 2tr in same place, ch1, skip 2 sts, *(2dtr, ch2, 2dtr) in next st**, [ch1, skip 2 sts, 3tr in next st] twice, ch1, skip 2 sts; rep from * twice more, then from * to ** once, ch1, skip 2 sts, 3tr in next st, ch1, sl st in top of beg ch3. End colour D. (40 sts, 16 chsp)

Rnd 5: Join colour E in ch2sp, ch3 (counts as 1 tr), (tr, ch2, 2tr) in same place, *tr in each st and ch1sp to next ch2sp, (2tr, ch2, 2tr) in ch2sp; rep from * twice more, tr in each st and ch1sp to end, sl st in top of beg ch3. (68 sts, 4 chsp)

Rnd 6: Ch1 and dc in same place, dc in next st, [3dc in ch2sp, dc in each st to next ch2sp] 3 times, 3dc in ch2sp, dc in each st to end, sl st in first dc made. End colour E. (80 sts)

Chart

- **Hook:** 5mm

- **Yarn:** DK; quantities below are per block (see also page 124)

- **Tension:** Each block = 15 x 30cm (6 x 12in)

- **Afghan size:** 105 x 150cm (42 x 60in); 35 blocks joined in 5 rows of 7 blocks

A: 5m (5.5yd)

B: 9m (9.9yd)

C: 11m (12.1yd)

D: 12m (13.2yd)

E: 13.5m (14.8yd)

F: 14.5m (15.9yd)

Granny Quilt

The granny square is an all-time favourite with crocheters. This design starts with a granny square, and then rows of double crochet are worked along one edge to make a rectangle. Try working the double crochet rows all in one colour for a patchwork effect. This afghan is finished with a double crochet edging, but the Granny edging on page 109 would also be a great choice.

Turn the page for the chart and pattern instructions.

Pattern

KEY

○ ch

• sl st

+ dc

⊤ tr

◄ begin round or row

Foundation ring: With colour A, ch4, sl st in first ch to form a ring.

Rnd 1: Ch3 (counts as 1 tr), 2tr in ring, [ch2, tr in ring] 3 times, ch2, sl st in top of beg ch3. End colour A. (12 sts)

Rnd 2: Join colour B in ch2sp, ch3 (counts as 1 tr), 2tr in same place, [ch1, (3tr, ch2, 3tr) in next ch2sp] 3 times, ch1, 3tr in next ch2sp, ch2, sl st in top of beg ch3. End colour B. (24 sts)

Rnd 3: Join colour C in ch2sp, ch3 (counts as 1 tr), 2tr in same place, *ch1, 3tr in next ch1sp, ch1**, (3tr, ch2, 3 tr) in ch2sp; rep from * twice more, then from * to ** once, 3tr in next ch2sp, ch2, sl st in top of beg ch3. End colour C. (36 sts)

Rnd 4: Join colour D in ch2sp, ch3 (counts as 1 tr), 2tr in same place, *[ch1, 3tr in next ch1sp] twice, ch1**, (3tr, ch2, 3 tr) in ch2sp; rep from * twice more, then from * to ** once, 3tr in next ch2sp, ch2, sl st in top of beg ch3. End colour D. (48 sts)

Rnd 5: Join colour E in ch2sp, ch3 (counts as 1 tr), 2tr in same place, *[ch1, 3tr in next ch1sp] 3 times, ch1**, (3tr, ch2, 3tr) in ch2sp; rep from * twice more, then from * to ** once, 3tr in next ch2sp, ch2, sl st in top of beg ch3. End colour E. (60 sts)

Rnd 6: Join colour F in ch2sp, ch3 (counts as 1 tr), 2tr in same place, *[ch1, 3tr in next ch1sp] 4 times, ch1**, (3tr, ch2, 3tr) in ch2sp; rep from * twice more, then from * to ** once, 3tr in next ch2sp, ch2, sl st in top of beg ch3. End colour F. (72 sts)

Row 7: Join colour B, ch1 and dc in same place, dc in each st and ch to next corner ch2sp, dc in ch2sp, turn. (25 sts)

Row 8: Ch 1, dc in each st to end. End colour B. Turn.

Rows 9 + 10: Repeat row 8 using colour C.

Rows 11 + 12: Repeat row 8 using colour D.

Rows 13 + 14: Repeat row 8 using colour E.

Rows 15 + 16: Repeat row 8 using colour F.

Rows 17 + 18: Repeat row 8 using colour A.

Rows 19 + 20: Repeat row 8 using colour F.

Rows 21 + 22: Repeat row 8 using colour E.

Rows 23 + 24: Repeat row 8 using colour D.

Rows 25 + 26: Repeat row 8 using colour C.

Rows 27 + 28: Repeat row 8 using colour B.

To make throw: Make 35 blocks and sew together in 5 rows of 7 blocks, alternating direction of rectangles.

Edging: With colour F, work dc in each st and row end along each side and 3dc in each corner.

Chart

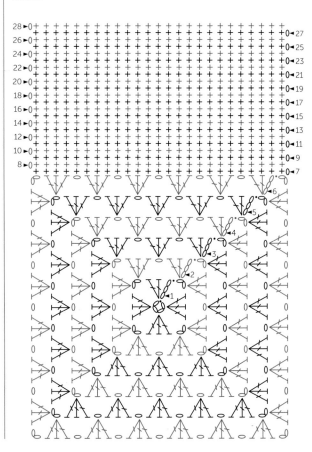

Try working a couple of the double crochet rows in a fluffy yarn for some added interest. Although novelty yarns are trickier to work with, this pattern is a great opportunity for a little experimentation.

- **Hook:** 5mm

- **Yarn:** DK (see page 124 for quantities)

- **Tension:** Approx. 14½ sts and 16 rows in dc = 10cm (4in) square

- **Reversible**

A

B

C

D

E

F

KEY

o   ch

+   dc

)   dc in place indicated

◄   begin row

Purpilicious

This lovely open design looks the same on both sides and is quick to work up. Try using just two colours for a bold and striking throw.

Pattern

Foundation row: With colour A, ch a multiple of 5 + 3 + 1 turning ch.

Row 1: Beg in 2nd ch from hook, dc in each ch to end, turn.

Row 2: Ch1, dc in each st to end, turn.

Row 3: Ch1, dc in first st, [dc in next st, ch4, skip 4 sts] to last 2 sts, dc in last 2 sts. End colour A. Turn.

Row 4: Join colour B, ch1, dc in first st, ch1, skip 1 st, [4dc in ch4sp, ch1, skip 1 st] to last st, dc in last st, turn.

Row 5: Ch1, dc in first st, [ch1, skip ch1sp, dc in next 4 sts] to last ch1sp and last st, ch1, skip ch1sp, dc in last st. End colour B. Turn.

Row 6: Join colour A, ch1, dc in first st, dc in skipped st 3 rows below, working around ch of previous 2 rows, [ch4, skip 4 sts,

dc in skipped st 3 rows below, working around ch of previous 2 rows] to last st, dc in last st, turn.

Row 7: Ch1, dc in first st, [dc in next st, 4dc in ch4sp] to last 2 sts, dc in last 2 sts, turn.

Rows 8 + 9: Repeat rows 2 + 3. End colour A. Turn.

Rows 10 + 11: Repeat rows 4 + 5 using colour C.

Rows 12–15: Repeat rows 6–9 using colour A.

Repeat rows 10–15, changing colour used for rows 10 + 11 as follows: colour D, colour E, colour F.

Continue repeating rows 10–15 in established colour sequence until fabric is the desired length. End with a row 14 (2 rows of dc in colour A).

Chart

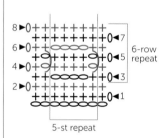

6-row repeat

5-st repeat

- **Hook:** 5mm

- **Yarn:** DK (see page 124 for quantities)

- **Tension:** 16 sts and 14 rows = 10cm (4in) square

A

B

C

D

KEY

o   ch

+   dc

⌠   dc in place indicated

T   htr

🔵   bobble

◄   begin row

Bobble Band

Bands of double crochet and tactile bobble stitches lie on a bed of half treble crochet in this design. The pattern is easy to remember and works up quickly. Use colours to match your decor, or go crazy with colour and work the bands in different colourways on a neutral background.

Pattern

Foundation row: With colour A, ch a multiple of 4 + 3 + 2 turning ch.

Row 1 (RS): Beg in 4th ch from hook (first ch2 counts as 1 htr), htr in each ch to end, turn.

Row 2 (WS): Ch2 (counts as 1 htr), htr in each st to end, turn.

Rows 3–5: Repeat row 2. End colour A.

Row 6: Join colour B, ch1, dc in each st to end. End colour B. Turn.

Row 7: Repeat row 6 using colour C.

Row 8: Repeat row 6 using colour D.

Row 9: Repeat row 6 using colour A.

Row 10: Join colour C, ch1, dc in first 2 sts, [ch1, skip 1 st, BO in next st, ch1, skip 1 st, dc in next st] to last st, dc in last st. End colour C. Turn.

Row 11: Join colour A, ch1, dc in first st, [dc in next st, dc in next skipped st 2 rows below, dc in BO, dc in next skipped st 2 rows below]

to last 2 sts, dc in last 2 sts. End colour A. Turn.

Row 12: Repeat row 6 using colour D.

Row 13: Repeat row 6 using colour C.

Row 14: Repeat row 6 using colour B.

Row 15: Repeat row 2 using colour A.

Repeat rows 2–15 until fabric is the desired length. End with a row 5 (5 rows of htr in colour A).

Chart

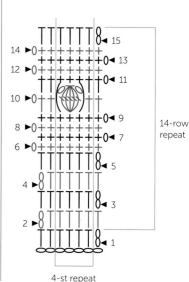

14-row repeat

4-st repeat

Special Stitch

Bobble (BO):
Work 5tr in place indicated but omit final yo of each tr, yo and pull through all 6 loops on hook.

- **Hook:** 5mm

- **Yarn:** DK (see page 124 for quantities)

- **Tension:** Approx. 13½ sts and 10 rows = 10cm (4in) square

A

B

C

D

KEY

○   ch

+   dc

T   htr

   bobble

◀   begin row

Bibbledy Bobbledy Blue

Comprised mainly of half treble crochet stitches, this design works up quite quickly. Rows of double crochet stitches and tactile bobble stitches add some colour. Try working each band of double crochet and bobble stitches in a different colourway each time you repeat it.

Pattern

Foundation row: With colour A, ch a multiple of 4 + 3 + 2 turning ch.

Row 1 (RS): Beg in 4th ch from hook (first ch2 counts as 1 htr), htr in each ch to end, turn.

Row 2 (WS): Ch2 (count as 1 htr), htr in each st to end, turn.

Rows 3–5: Repeat row 2. End colour A.

Row 6: Join colour B, ch1, dc in each st to end. End colour B. Turn.

Row 7: Repeat row 6 using colour C.

Row 8: Join colour D, ch1 and dc in first st, [dc in next st, ch1, skip 1 st, BO in next st, ch1, skip 1 st] to last 2 sts, dc in last 2 sts. End colour D. Turn.

Row 9: Join colour C, ch1, dc in first 2 sts, [dc in skipped st 2 rows below, dc in BO, dc in skipped st 2 rows below, dc in next st] to last st, dc in last st. End colour C. Turn.

Row 10: Repeat row 6 using colour B.

Rows 11–15: Repeat row 2 using colour A. End colour A.

Row 16: Repeat row 6 using colour C.

Row 17: Repeat row 2 using colour D. End colour D.

Row 18: Repeat row 6 using colour C.

Row 19: Repeat row 2 using colour A.

Repeat rows 2–19 until fabric is the desired length.

Sample is shown with Flounce edging (page 107)

SPECIAL STITCH

Bobble (BO):
Work 5tr in place indicated but omit final yo of each tr, yo and pull through all 6 loops on hook.

Chart

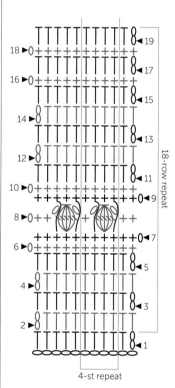

18-row repeat

4-st repeat

- **Hook:** 5mm

- **Yarn:** DK (see page 124 for quantities)

- **Tension:** 10 sts and 12½ rows = 10cm (4in) square

- **Reversible**

A

B

C

D

E

KEY

o ch

+ dc

† tr

✕ X-st

◄ begin row

Crossed Hatch

This lacy pattern works up quickly and is a great way to use up scraps of different coloured yarns for a really colourful blanket. Or try alternating two rows worked in a plain colour with two rows worked in variegated or self-striping yarn.

Pattern

Foundation row: With colour A, ch a multiple of 2 + 2 + 1 turning ch.

Row 1: Beg in 2nd ch from hook, dc in each ch to end, turn.

Row 2: Ch3 (counts as 1 tr), [X-st in next 2 sts] to last st, tr in last st, turn.

Row 3: Ch1, dc in each st to end. End colour A. Turn.

Row 4: Join colour B, ch1, dc in each st to end, turn.

Row 5: Ch3 (counts as 1 tr), [X-st in next 2 sts] to last st, tr in last st, turn.

Row 6: Ch1, dc in each st to end. End colour B. Turn.

Rows 7–9: Repeat rows 4–6 using colour C.

Rows 10–12: Repeat rows 4–6 using colour D.

Rows 13–15: Repeat rows 4–6 using colour E.

Rows 16–18: Repeat rows 4–6 using colour A.

Repeat rows 4–18 until fabric is the desired length.

Chart

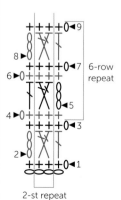

6-row repeat

2-st repeat

SPECIAL STITCH

Cross stitch (X-st): Skip 1 st, tr in next st, tr in skipped st.

- **Hook:** 5mm
- **Yarn:** DK; quantities below are per block (see also page 124)
- **Tension:** Each block = 15cm (6in) square

A: 4m (4.4yd)

B: 6m (6.6yd)

C: 6m (6.6yd)

D: 6m (6.6yd)

E: 6m (6.6yd)

F: 20m (21.9yd)

KEY

- o ch
- • sl st
- + dc
- ⊥ Ext dc
- T htr
- ⊤ tr
- ⊤ dtr
- popcorn
- ◄ begin round

Flower Patch

This block is comprised of four little squares that are sewn together. Each little square could also be used to edge a blanket. Try working each square with a different background colour for a patchwork effect.

Pattern

For each block make 4 squares – 1 each using colours B, C, D and E for round 2.

Foundation ring: With colour A, ch4, sl st in first ch to form a ring.

Rnd 1: Ch1, 8Ext dc in ring, sl st in first Ext dc made. End colour A. (8 sts)

Rnd 2: Join colour B, C, D or E, *(ch3, PC) in same place, ch3, sl st in next st; rep from * 7 times more, working last sl st in base of first PC made. End colour. (8 PC)

Rnd 3: Join colour F in top of PC, ch1 and dc in same place, *(ch3, dc in top of next PC, ch4**, dc in top of next PC; rep from * twice more, then from * to ** once, sl st in first dc made. (8 sts, 8 chsp)

Rnd 4: Ch2 (counts as 1 htr), *3dc in ch3sp, htr in next st, (htr, tr, dtr, tr, htr) in ch4sp**, htr in next st;

Chart

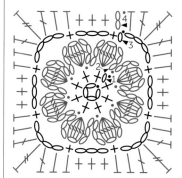

rep from * twice more, then from * to ** once, sl st in top of beg ch2. End colour F. (40 sts)

Join squares together by sewing through back loops of sts using colour F.

Sample is shown with Prism edging (page 109).

SPECIAL STITCHES

Extended double crochet (Ext dc):
Insert hook in place indicated and draw up a loop (2 loops on hook), ch1, yo and pull through both loops on hook.

Popcorn (PC):
Work 5tr in place indicated, remove hook from loop, insert hook from front to back in top of first tr, pick up dropped loop and pull through loop on hook.

- **Hook:** 5mm

- **Yarn:** DK; quantities below are per block (see also page 124)

- **Tension:** Each block = 15cm (6in) square

A: 6m (6.6yd)

B: 6m (6.6yd)

C: 6m (6.6yd)

D: 8.5m (9.3yd)

E: 16.5m (18.1yd)

KEY

- ⟲ magic ring
- o ch
- • sl st
- + dc
- ⨾ BPdc
- ⊤ htr
- ⊺ tr
- ⨎ W-st
- ◄ begin round

Folk Flower

Inspired by folk art, this little flower block is tactile and bright. The waistcoat stitches on the last round are easy to do and create the look of knitted stitches, but you could replace these with normal double crochet stitches if you prefer.

Pattern

Foundation ring: With colour A, make a magic ring.

Rnd 1: Ch1, 8dc in ring, sl st in first dc made. End colour A. (8 sts)

Rnd 2: Join colour B, ch1, 2dc in each st around, sl st in first dc made. End colour B. (16 sts)

Rnd 3: Join colour C, ch1, 2dc in each st around, sl st in first dc made. End colour C. (32 sts)

Rnd 4: Join colour D, ch3 (counts as 1 tr), tr in same place, ch3, sl st in next st, [sl st in next st, ch3, 2tr in each of next 2 sts, ch3, sl st in next st] 7 times, sl st in next st, ch3, 2tr in next st, sl st in top of beg ch3. End colour D. (8 petals)

Rnd 5: Join colour E in next sl st between petals, ch3 (counts as 1 tr), *BPdc in next 4 sts, (tr, ch2, tr) in sl st between petals, BPdc in next 4 sts**, tr in sl st between petals; rep from * twice more, then from * to ** once, sl st in top of beg ch3. (44 sts, 4 chsp)

Rnd 6: Ch3 (counts as 1 tr), tr in next 5 sts, *(2tr, ch2, 2tr) in ch2sp**, tr in next 11 sts; rep from * twice more, then from * to ** once, tr in next 5 sts, sl st in top of beg ch3. End colour E. (60 sts, 4 chsp)

Rnd 7: Join colour A in corner ch2sp, ch1, *(dc, htr, dc) in ch2sp, BPdc in next 15 sts; rep from * 3 times more, sl st in first dc made. End colour A. (72 sts)

Chart

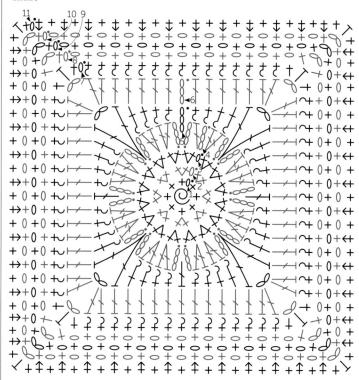

Rnd 8: Join colour D in corner htr, ch1, *(dc, ch2, dc) in htr, [ch1, skip 1 st, dc in next st] 8 times, ch1, skip 1 st; rep from * 3 times more, sl st in first dc made. End colour D. (40 sts, 40 chsp)

Rnd 9: Join colour C in corner ch2sp, ch1, *(dc, ch2, dc) in ch2sp, [ch1, skip 1 st, dc in next ch1sp] 9 times, ch1, skip 1 st; rep from * 3 times more, sl st in first dc made. End colour C. (44 sts, 44 chsp)

Rnd 10: Join colour B in corner ch2sp, ch1, *(dc, ch2, dc) in ch2sp, [ch1, skip 1 st, dc in next st] 10 times, ch1, skip 1 st; rep from * 3 times more, sl st in first dc made. End colour B. (48 sts, 48 chsp)

Rnd 11: Join colour E in ch2sp, ch1, *(dc, htr, dc) in ch2sp, W-st in each st and dc in each ch1sp to next corner ch2sp; rep from * 3 times more, sl st in first dc made. End colour E. (104 sts)

SPECIAL STITCH

Insert hook between vertical V-shaped strands at front of
indicated st and work dc.

- **Hook:** 5mm

- **Yarn:** DK; quantities below are per block (see also page 124)

- **Tension:** Each block = 15cm (6in) square

A: 2.5m (2.8yd)

B: 6m (6.6yd)

C: 6.5m (7.2yd)

D: 5m (5.5yd)

E: 7m (7.7yd)

KEY

○ ch

• sl st

+ dc

T htr

╀ tr

╪ dtr

⋀ dc3tog

⋀ tr2tog

◀ begin round

knotty but Nice

Reminiscent of Celtic knotwork designs, this block has a striking geometric look. Try working in black, white and greys for a bold throw. If your chain stitches are too loose or too tight, round 2 may cause puckering, so feel free to increase or decrease the number of chains if necessary.

Pattern

Foundation ring: With colour A, ch4, sl st in first ch to form a ring.

Rnd 1: Ch3 (counts as 1 tr), 2tr in ring, [ch10, 3tr in ring] 3 times, ch10, sl st in top of beg ch3. End colour A. (12 sts, 4 chsp)

Rnd 2: Join colour B in ch10sp, ch3 (counts as 1 tr), (5tr, ch2, 6tr) in same place, *dc3tog in next 3 sts, (6tr, ch2, 6tr) in next ch10sp; rep from * twice more, dc3tog in next 3 sts, sl st in top of beg ch3. End colour B. (52 sts, 4 chsp)

Rnd 3: Join colour C in ch2sp, ch3 (counts as 1 tr), (2tr, ch2, 3tr) in same place, *tr in next 4 sts, skip 2 sts, dtr in dc3tog, skip 2 sts, tr in next 4 sts**, (3tr, ch2, 3tr) in ch2sp; rep from * twice more, then from * to ** once, sl st in top of beg ch3. End colour C. (60 sts, 4 chsp)

Rnd 4: Join colour D in ch2sp, ch1, *(dc, htr, dc) in ch2sp, dc in next 3 sts, htr in next 3 sts, tr2tog, htr in next 3 sts, dc in next 3 sts; rep from * 3 times more, sl st in first dc made. End colour D. (64 sts)

Rnd 5: Join colour E in corner htr, ch2 (counts as 1 htr), (tr, htr) in same place, *htr in each st to next corner htr, (htr, tr, htr) in corner htr; rep from * twice more, htr in each st to end, sl st in top of beg ch2. End colour E. (72 sts)

Chart

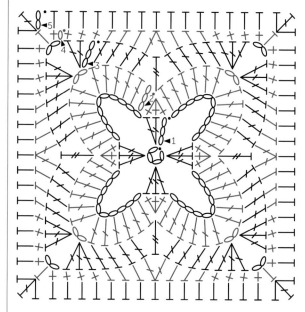

SPECIAL STITCHES

Double crochet 3 together (dc3tog):
Work dc in each of next 3 sts but omit final yo of each dc, yo and pull through all 4 loops on hook.

Treble crochet 2 together (tr2tog):
Work tr in next tr but omit final yo, skip dtr, work another incomplete tr in next tr, yo and pull through all 3 loops on hook.

Skill level: 3

- **Hook:** 5mm

- **Yarn:** DK; quantities below are per block (see also page 124)

- **Tension:** Each block = 15cm (6in) square

- **Afghan size:** 90cm (36in) square; 36 blocks joined in 6 rows of 6 blocks

A: 3m (3.3yd)

B: 6m (6.6yd)

C: 17m (18.6yd)

D: 6.5m (7.2yd)

E: 6.5m (7.2yd)

F: 6.5m (7.2yd)

G: 6.5m (7.2yd)

Roisin Baby Blanket

Using the traditional Irish rose as a starting point, this block is packed with tactile loveliness, and the 3D flowers make the finished blanket deliciously chunky. You can work the petal rounds all in one colour or even try different colours for each block.

Turn the page for the chart and pattern instructions.

Chart

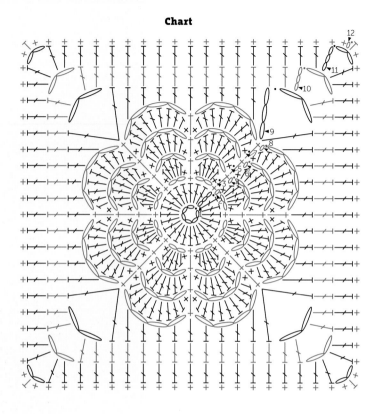

KEY

- ⊙ ch
- • sl st
- + dc
- ⊤ htr
- ⊤ tr
- ◄ begin round

Pattern

Foundation ring: With colour A, ch6, sl st in first ch to form a ring.

Rnd 1: Ch3 (counts as 1 tr), 23tr in ring, sl st in top of beg ch3. End colour A. (24 sts)

Rnd 2: Join colour B, ch1 and dc in same place, [ch2, skip 2 sts, dc in next st] 7 times, ch2, skip 2 sts, sl st in first dc made. (8 sts)

Rnd 3: [(Dc, htr, 3tr, htr, dc) in ch2sp] 8 times, sl st in first dc made. End colour B. (56 sts)

Rnd 4: Fold petals of last round forwards and work into sts of round 2: join colour C in dc on round 2, ch1 and dc in same place, [ch3, dc in next dc] 7 times, ch3, sl st in first dc made. (8 sts)

Rnd 5: [(Dc, htr, 5tr, htr, dc) in ch3sp] 8 times, sl st in first dc made. (72 sts)

Rnd 6: Fold petals of last round forwards and work into sts of round 4: [dc in next dc, ch4] 8 times, sl st in first dc made. (8 sts)

Rnd 7: [(Dc, htr, 7tr, htr, dc) in ch4sp] 8 times, sl st in first dc made. End colour C. (88 sts)

Rnd 8: Fold petals of last round forwards and work into sts of round 6: join colour D in dc on round 6, ch1 and dc in same place, [ch4, dc in next dc] 7 times, ch4, sl st in first dc made. (8 sts)

Rnd 9: Ch3 (counts as 1 tr), *4tr in ch4sp, tr in next dc, 4tr in ch4sp**, (tr, ch2, tr) in next st; rep from * twice more, then from * to ** once, tr in first st, ch2, sl st in top of beg ch3. (44 sts)

Rnd 10: Ch3 (counts as 1 tr), tr in same place, [tr in each st to next corner ch2sp, (2tr, ch2, 2tr) in ch2sp] 3 times, tr in each st to first corner ch2sp, 2tr in ch2sp, ch2, sl st in top of beg ch3. (60 sts)

Rnd 11: Repeat round 10. (76 sts)

Rnd 12: Ch1, dc in same place, [dc in each st to next corner ch2sp, (dc, htr, dc) in ch2sp] 3 times, dc in each st to first corner ch2sp, (dc, htr) in ch2sp, sl st in first dc made. End colour D. (88 sts)

To make baby blanket: Make 36 blocks, working 9 blocks each using colours D, E, F and G for rounds 8–12. Join with a crochet seam, arranging the blocks in any colour order you wish. Add Curvy edging (page 104).

The 3D flowers make this a thick and cosy blanket. For a more delicate afghan, try working in a lighter weight yarn, but remember that yarn quantities will be different if you do so.

Skill level: 3

- **Hook:** 5mm
- **Yarn:** DK (see page 124 for quantities)
- **Tension:** 14 sts and 5¾ rows = 10cm (4in) square

A
B
C
D
E
F

KEY

○	ch	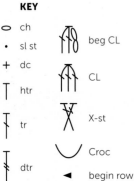 beg CL	
•	sl st		
+	dc	CL	
⊤	htr		
⊤	tr	X X-st	
⊤	dtr	‿ Croc	
		◄ begin row	

Pond

This watery design features offset crocodile stitches to create tactile leaves, and cluster stitches to form flower heads. Keep an eye on when to turn the work.

Pattern

Foundation row: With colour A, ch a multiple of 7 + 1 + 3 turning ch.

Row 1 (RS): Beg in 5th ch from hook (first ch3 counts as 1 tr), tr in each ch to end, turn.

Row 2 (WS): Ch3 (counts as 1 tr), tr in each st to end, turn.

Row 3: Repeat row 2. End colour A.

Row 4: Join colour B, ch5 (counts as 1 tr, ch2), skip 3 sts, tr in gap before next st, [ch2, skip 3 sts, 2tr in next st, ch2, skip 3 sts, tr in gap before next st] to last 4 sts, ch2, skip 3 sts, tr in last st, turn.

Row 5: Sl st in first st, ch2, [sl st in next st, Croc over next 2 sts] to last 2 sts, sl st in next st, ch2, sl st in last st. End colour B. Turn.

Row 6: Join colour C, ch5 (counts as 1 tr, ch2), 2tr in next sl st, ch2, [tr in centre of Croc, ch2, 2tr in next sl st, ch2] to last st, tr in last sl st, turn.

Row 7: Sl st in first st, [Croc over next 2 sts, sl st in next st] to end. End colour C. Do not turn.

Row 8: Join colour D in first sl st of last row, ch1, dc in first sl st, [9tr in centre of next Croc, dc in next sl st] to end. End colour D. Do not turn.

Row 9: Join colour E in first tr of row 8, beg CL, [ch3, CL] twice, ch3, skip 1 st, *[CL, ch3] 3 times, skip 1 st; rep from * to last 10 sts, [CL, ch3] twice, CL, skip last st. End colour E. Do not turn.

Row 10: Join colour F in first dc of row 8, ch4 (counts as 1 dtr), *(htr, 2dc) in next ch3sp, (2dc, htr) in next ch3sp, dtr in next skipped st on row 8; rep from * to end, turn.

Row 11: Repeat row 2.

Row 12: Ch3 (counts as 1 tr), *[X-st] 3 times, tr in next st; rep from * to end. End colour F. Do not turn.

Row 13: Join colour A in first st of last row, ch3 (counts as 1 tr), *[X-st] 3 times, tr in next st; rep from * to end, turn.

Rows 14 + 15: Repeat row 2.

Repeat rows 2–15 until fabric is the desired length.

Chart

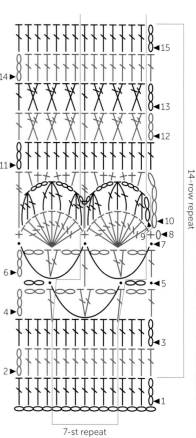

14-row repeat

7-st repeat

SPECIAL STITCHES

Crocodile stitch (Croc):
5tr around next tr, working from top to bottom of post; 5tr around next tr, working from bottom to top of post.

Beginning cluster (beg CL):
Ch2, work tr in each of next 2 sts but omit final yo of each tr, yo and pull through all 3 loops on hook.

Cluster (CL):
Work tr each of next 3 sts but omit final yo of each tr, yo and pull through all 4 loops on hook.

Cross stitch (X-st):
Skip 1 st, tr in next st, tr in skipped st.

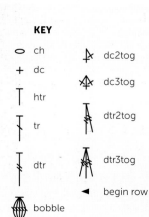

■ **Skill level:** 2

■ **Hook:** 5mm

■ **Yarn:** DK (see page 124 for quantities)

■ **Tension:** 12 sts and 9½ rows = 10cm (4in) square

A

B

C

D

E

F

KEY

o   ch

+   dc

T   htr

⊤   tr

⊥   dtr

❂   bobble

⋀   dc2tog

⋀   dc3tog

⋀   dtr2tog

⋀   dtr3tog

◄   begin row

Snakes and Ladders

This bright design is reminiscent of the childhood board game, and would be a great afghan for a toddler. Try working in natural colours for an earthy afghan for the home. Keep an eye on when to turn the work.

Pattern

Foundation row: With colour A, ch a multiple of 6 + 1 + 3 turning ch.

Row 1: Beg in 5th ch from hook (first ch3 counts as 1 tr), tr in each ch to end. End colour A. Do not turn.

Row 2: Join colour B in first st of last row, ch3 (counts as 1 tr), tr in each st to end. End colour B. Do not turn.

Row 3: Repeat row 2 using colour C. End colour C. Turn.

Row 4: Join colour D, ch1, dc in first 3 sts, [BO in next st, dc in next 2 sts] to last st, dc in last st. End colour D. Turn.

Row 5: Join colour C, ch3 (counts as 1 tr), tr in each st to end. End colour C. Do not turn.

Row 6: Join colour B in first st of last row and repeat row 5. End colour B. Do not turn.

Row 7: Join colour A in first st of last row and repeat row 5. End colour A. Turn.

Row 8: Join colour D, ch1, dc in each st to end. End colour D. Turn.

Row 9: Join colour E, ch1, dc in first st, *htr in next st, tr in next st, 3tr in next st, tr in next st, htr in next st, dc in next st; rep from * to end. End colour E. Turn.

Row 10: Join colour F, ch1, dc2tog in first 2 sts, *dc in next 2 sts, 3dc in next st, dc in next 2 sts**, dc3tog; rep from * to last 7 sts, rep from * to ** once, dc2tog in last 2 sts. End colour F. Turn.

Row 11: Repeat row 10 using colour D.

Row 12: Repeat row 10 using colour F.

Row 13: Join colour E, ch3, dtr in next st, *tr in next st, htr in next st, dc in next st, htr in next st, tr in next st**, dtr3tog; rep from * to last 7 sts, rep from * to ** once, dtr2tog in last 2 sts. End colour E. Turn.

Row 14: Join colour D, ch1, dc in each st to end. End colour D. Turn

Row 15: Repeat row 5 using colour A.

Repeat rows 2–15 until fabric is the desired length.

Sample is shown with Curvy edging (page 104).

Chart

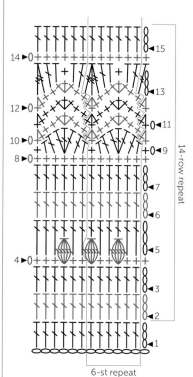

SPECIAL STITCHES

Bobble (BO):
Work 5tr in place indicated but omit final yo of each tr, yo and pull through all 6 loops on hook.

Double crochet 2 together (dc2tog):
Work dc in each of next 2 sts but omit final yo of each dc, yo and pull through all 3 loops on hook.

Double crochet 3 together (dc3tog):
Work dc in each of next 3 sts but omit final yo of each dc, yo and pull through all 4 loops on hook.

Double treble 2 together (dtr2tog):
Work dtr in each of next 2 sts but omit final yo of each dtr, yo and pull through all 3 loops on hook.

Double treble 3 together (dtr3tog):
Work dtr in each of next 3 sts but omit final yo of each dtr, yo and pull through all 4 loops on hook.

- **Hook:** 5mm

- **Yarn:** DK; quantities below are per block (see also page 124)

- **Tension:** Each block = 15cm (6in) square

- **Crochet techinique:** Tapestry (page 119)

- **Reversible**

A: 23m (25.2yd)

B: 11m (12.1yd)

Tile

This simple block uses just two colours. On the middle section of the block, carry the unused colour along the wrong side and work double crochet over it. Try laying out squares in opposite directions to create an interesting pattern.

Pattern

Foundation row: With colour A, ch22 + 1 turning ch.

Working from chart: Start at the bottom right-hand corner of the chart and work in double crochet, beginning the first row in the 2nd ch from hook. Each square represents 1 stitch. Right-side rows are read from right to left and wrong-side rows are read from left to right. Remember to ch1 at the beginning of each row for a turning ch (this does not count as a stitch).

To change to a different colour in the middle of a row: Work to 1 stitch before the colour change. Begin this stitch normally, working to the last yarn over, then drop the current colour to the wrong side of the work, pick up the new colour and use it to complete the stitch. Hold the unused colour along the top edge and work double crochet over it.

Chart

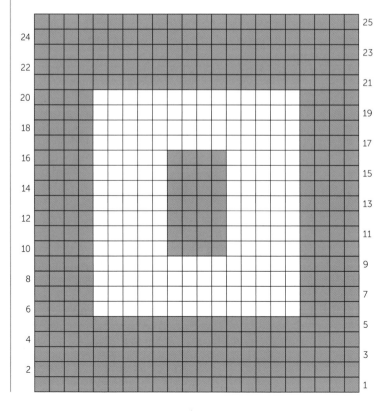

- **Hook:** 5mm
- **Yarn:** DK; quantities below are per block (see also page 124)
- **Tension:** Each block = 15cm (6in) square

A: 11m (12.1yd)

B: 8m (8.8yd)

C: 3.5m (3.9yd)

D: 11m (12.1yd)

KEY

o	ch
•	sl st
+	dc
T	htr
Ŧ	tr
	beg CL
	CL
◄	begin round

Tulips

This block starts as a circle of tulips by working V-stitches in green to create sepals and then cluster stitches on the following round to form the flower heads. A square border of tulips finishes the block.

Pattern

Foundation ring: With colour A, ch5, sl st in first ch to form a ring.

Rnd 1: Ch1, 16dc in ring, sl st in first dc made. End colour A. (16 sts)

Rnd 2: Join colour B, ch4 (counts as 1 tr, ch1), tr in same place, [skip 1 st, V-st in next st] 7 times, sl st in 3rd ch of beg ch4. End colour B. (16 sts, 8 chsp)

Rnd 3: Join colour C in next ch1sp, beg CL in same place, [ch4, skip 2 sts, CL in ch1sp] 7 times, ch4, sl st in top of beg CL. End colour C. (8 CL, 8 chsp)

Rnd 4: Join colour A in next ch4sp, ch2 (counts as 1 htr), (htr, dc, 2htr) in same place, *(htr, 2tr, ch2, 2tr, htr) in next ch4sp**, (2htr, dc, 2htr) in next ch4sp; rep from * twice more, then from * to ** once, sl st in top of beg ch2. End colour A. (44 sts, 4 chsp)

Rnd 5: Join colour B in next corner ch2sp, ch4 (counts as 1 tr, ch1), (tr, ch1, tr) in same place, *[skip 1 st, V-st in next st] 5 times**, ([tr, ch1] twice, tr) in corner ch2sp; rep from * twice more, then from * to ** once, sl st in 3rd ch of beg ch4. End colour B. (52 sts, 28 chsp)

Rnd 6: Join colour D in next ch1sp, beg CL in same place, *ch5, CL in next ch1sp, [ch2, skip 2 sts, CL in next ch1sp] 6 times; rep from * twice more, ch5, CL in next ch1sp, [ch2, skip 2 sts, CL in next ch1sp] 5 times, sl st in top of beg CL. End colour D. (28 CL, 28 chsp)

Rnd 7: Join colour A in corner ch5sp, ch1, *(2dc, htr, 2dc) in ch5sp, [3dc in ch2sp] 6 times; rep from * 3 times more, sl st in first dc made. End colour A. (92 sts)

Chart

- **Hook:** 5mm
- **Yarn:** DK (see page 124 for quantities)
- **Tension:** 14 sts and 8 rows = 10cm (4in) square
- **Reversible**

A

B

C

D

E

KEY

o   ch

+   dc

T   htr

†   tr

‡   dtr

◀   begin row

Wavy

This simple design comprised of straight and wavy rows is a great beginner project. It would look beautiful in all sorts of different colourways.

Pattern

Foundation row: With colour A, ch a multiple of 14 + 13 + 3 turning ch.

Row 1: Beg in 5th ch from hook (first ch3 counts as 1 tr), tr in each ch to end, turn.

Row 2: Ch3 (counts as 1 tr), tr in each st to end. End colour A. Turn.

Rows 3 + 4: Repeat row 2 using colour B.

Rows 5 + 6: Repeat row 2 using colour C.

Row 7: Join colour D, ch1, dc in first st, *htr in next 2 sts, tr in next 2 sts, dtr in next 3 sts, tr in next 2 sts, htr in next 2 sts**, dc in next 3 sts; rep from * to last 12 sts, rep from * to ** once, dc in last st. End colour D. Turn.

Row 8: Join colour E, ch4 (counts as 1 dtr), tr in next 2 sts, htr in next 2 sts, dc in next 3 sts, htr in next 2 sts, tr in next 2 sts, *dtr in next 3 sts, tr in next 2 sts, htr in next 2 sts, dc in next 3 sts, htr in next 2 sts, tr in next 2 sts; rep from * to last st, dtr in last st. End colour E. Turn.

Rows 9–12: Repeat rows 7 + 8 twice more.

Row 13: Join colour A, ch3 (counts as 1 tr), tr in each st to end, turn.

Repeat rows 2–13 until fabric is the desired length.

Sample is shown with Mosaic edging (page 106).

Chart

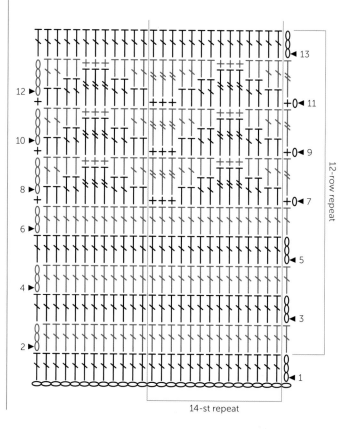

12-row repeat

14-st repeat

- **Hook:** 5mm

- **Yarn:** DK; quantities below are per block (see also page 124)

- **Tension:** Each block = 10cm (4in) square

- **Reversible**

A: 9.5m (10.4yd)

B: 10m (11yd)

C: 3.5m (3.9yd)

D: 18.5m (20.3yd)

KEY

o	ch
•	sl st
+	dc
T	htr
ꝼ	tr
ꝼ	BPtr
ꝼ	dtr
◄	begin round

Purple Petal Eater

Use bright colours for the flowers and a neutral shade for the background to create a really colourful afghan. You could also try working the flowers in lighter shades on bright backgrounds.

Pattern

Foundation ring: With colour A, ch5, sl st in first ch to form a ring.

Rnd 1: Ch1, 16dc in ring, sl st in first dc made. End colour A. (16 sts)

Rnd 2: Join colour B, ch3 (counts as 1 tr), tr in same place, [2tr in next st] 15 times, sl st in top of beg ch3. End colour B. (32 sts)

Rnd 3: Join colour A in gap between 2tr, ch1 and dc in same place, [dc in gap before next st] 31 times, sl st in first dc made. End colour A. (32 sts)

Rnd 4: Join colour C in next st, ch1 and dc in same place, 3tr in next st, dc in next st, [skip 1 st, dc in next st, 3tr in next st, dc in next st] 7 times, skip 1 st, sl st in first dc made. End colour C. (40 sts)

Rnd 5: Join colour B in next st, ch2 (counts as 1 htr), tr in same place, 3tr in next st, (tr, htr) in next st, dc2tog in next 2 sts, *(htr, tr) in next st, 3tr in next st, (tr, htr) in next st, dc2tog in next 2 sts; rep from * 6 times more, sl st in top of beg ch2. End colour B. (64 sts)

Rnd 6: Join colour A, ch1 and dc in same place, 2dc in each of next 5 sts, dc in next st, *BPtr in skipped st on round 3, dc in next st, 2dc in each of next 5 sts, dc in next st; rep from * 6 times more, BPtr in skipped st on round 3, sl st in first dc made. End colour A. (104 sts)

Chart

Rnd 7: Fold petals forwards and join colour D in dc2tog on round 5, ch1 and dc in same place, *ch4, dc in next dc2tog on round 5, ch6**, dc in next dc2tog on round 5; rep from * twice more, then from * to ** once, sl st in first dc made. (8 sts, 8 chsp)

Rnd 8: Ch3 (counts as 1 tr), 3tr in ch4sp, *tr in next st, (4tr, ch2, 4tr) in ch6sp**, tr in next st, 4tr in ch4sp; rep from * twice more, then from * to ** once, sl st in top of beg ch3. (56 sts, 4 chsp)

Rnd 9: Ch3 (counts as 1 tr), *tr in each st to corner ch2sp, (tr, dtr, tr) in ch2sp; rep from * 3 times more, tr in each st to end, sl st in top of beg ch3. (68 sts)

Rnd 10: Ch1 and dc in same place, *dc in each st to corner dtr, (dc, htr, dc) in corner dtr; rep from * 3 times more, dc in each st to end, sl st in first dc made. End colour D. (76 sts)

SPECIAL STITCH

Double crochet 2 together (dc2tog):
Work dc in each of next 2 sts but omit
final yo of each dc, yo and pull through
all 3 loops on hook.

- **Hook:** 5mm

- **Yarn:** DK (see page 124 for quantities)

- **Tension:** Approx. 13½ sts and 6½ rows = 10cm (4in) square

A

B

C

D

E

F

KEY

o   ch

+   dc

⊤   tr

◄   begin row

Sideways

This is a lovely design because there is really only one row of instructions to remember. You could work the pattern in as many or as few colours as you like. The sample changes colour every row, but you could also work several rows in each colour.

Pattern

Foundation row: With colour A, ch a multiple of 4 + 5 + 4 turning ch.

Row 1 (RS): 3tr in 5th ch from hook, skip 3 ch, *(dc, ch3, 3tr) in next ch, skip 3 ch; rep from * to last ch, dc in last ch. End colour A. Turn.

Row 2 (WS): Join colour B, (ch4, 3tr) in first dc, *(dc, ch3, 3tr) in next ch3sp; rep from * to last ch4sp, dc in last ch4sp. End colour B. Turn.

Row 3: Repeat row 2 using colour C.

Row 4: Repeat row 2 using colour D.

Row 5: Repeat row 2 using colour E.

Row 6: Repeat row 2 using colour F.

Row 7: Repeat row 2 using colour A.

Repeat rows 2–7 until fabric is the desired length.

Last row: Join next colour in sequence, (ch4, 2tr) in first dc, *(dc, htr, tr) in next ch3sp; rep from * to last ch4sp, dc in last ch4sp. End colour.

Sample is shown with Spikes edging (page 105).

Chart

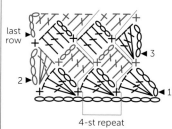

4-st repeat

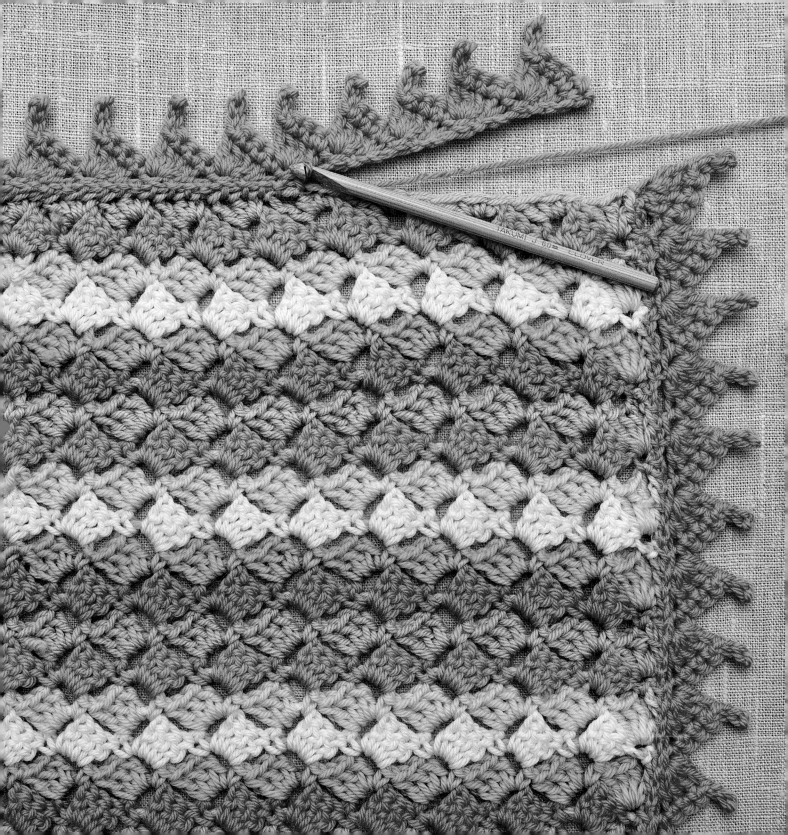

Skill level: 2

- **Hook:** 5mm

- **Yarn:** DK; quantities below are for afghan shown (see also page 124)

- **Tension:** Approx. 13½ sts and 21 rows = 10cm (4in) square

- **Afghan size:** 150 x 180cm (60 x 72in)

- **Reversible**

A: 720m (788yd)

B: 720m (788yd)

C: 720m (788yd)

D: 720m (788yd)

E: 720m (788yd)

F: 720m (788yd)

G: 720m (788yd)

Spiky Waves Throw

This is a simple but effective pattern. The sample shown has been made using a large colour palette, but the design would also look great worked in two colours. Take care not to work the spike stitches too tight, but also not too loose.

Turn the page for the chart and pattern instructions.

KEY

O   ch

+   dc

Ƨ   spike dc

◄   begin row

Pattern

Foundation row: With colour A, ch a multiple of 10 + 1 + 1 turning ch. To match afghan shown, ch202.

Row 1: Beg in 2nd ch from hook, dc in each ch to end, turn.

Rows 2–6: Ch1, dc in each st to end. End colour A. Turn.

Row 7: Join colour B, ch1, dc in first st, [spike dc 2 rows below, spike dc 3 rows below, spike dc 4 rows below, spike dc 5 rows below, spike dc 6 rows below, spike dc 5 rows below, spike dc 4 rows below, spike dc 3 rows below, spike dc 2 rows below, dc in next st] to end, turn.

Rows 8–12: Repeat rows 2–6. End colour B.

Row 13: Join colour C, ch1, dc in first st, [*spike dc 5 rows below, spike dc 4 rows below, spike dc 3 rows below, spike dc 2 rows below, dc in next st, spike dc 2 rows below, spike dc 3 rows below, spike dc 4 rows below, spike dc 5 rows below**, spike dc 6 rows below] to last 10 sts; rep from * to ** once more, dc in last st, turn.

Repeat rows 2–13 until fabric is the desired length, changing colour when instructed following the colour sequence A–G (42 rows to complete colour sequence).

To make the throw: Work 20 repeats across and repeat the colour sequence A–G nine times in total.

Chart

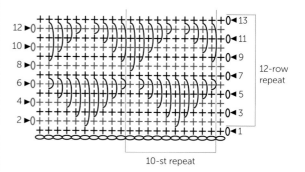

12-row repeat

10-st repeat

SPECIAL STITCH

Spike double crochet (spike dc): Insert hook in next st on specified row below the current row, yo and pull up a loop, lengthen loop to height of working row, yo and pull through both loops on hook.

You can use the same design to make matching cushions for your afghan. Start with a chain multiple that is long enough to cover the width of the cushion pad. Work as many rows as needed to cover both front and back of the cushion pad, and then sew up the three edges.

Edgings

Every afghan deserves a
beautiful edging, so here are
12 edging patterns for you to
choose from, using both sew-on
and crochet-on methods. Refer to
page 122 for more information
about edging techniques to get
the perfect finish.

Flowery page 107

Flounce page 107

Arches page 105

Spikes page 105

Crab page 105

Knitty page 104

Granny page 109

Prism page 109

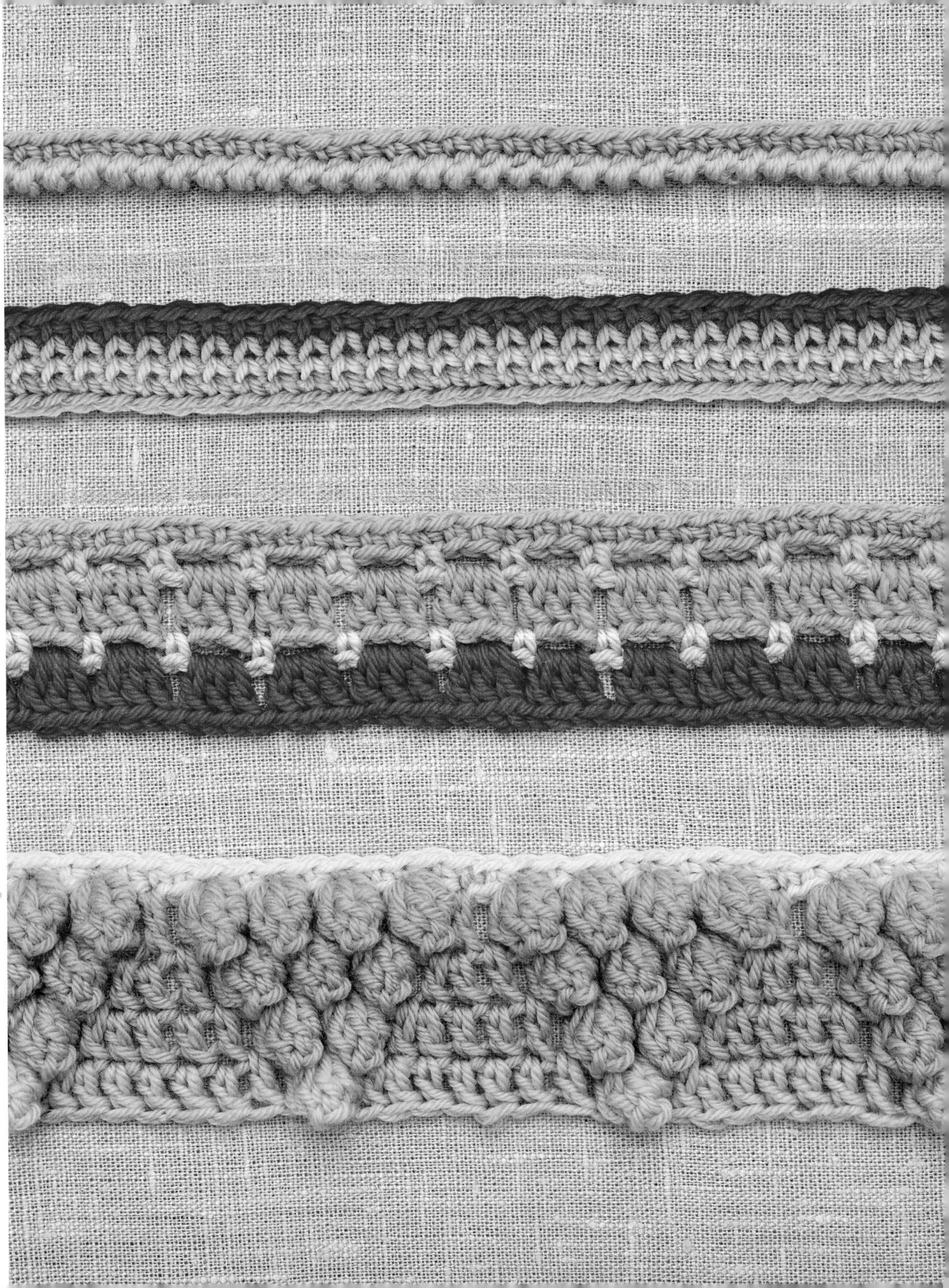

Knitty

A

B

C

Base round

KEY

○ ch

• sl st

+ dc

‡ W-st

◄ begin round

- **Hook:** 5mm
- **Yarn:** DK
- **Multiple:** Any number of sts
- **Technique:** Crochet-on (page 122)

Special stitch

Waistcoat stitch (W-st): Insert hook between vertical V-shaped strands at front of indicated st and work dc.

Pattern

Rnd 1: Join colour A in 2nd dc of any corner 3dc of base round, ch1, [3dc in corner st, W-st in each st to next corner st] 4 times, sl st in first dc made. End colour A.

Rnd 2: Join colour B in 2nd dc of corner 3dc, ch1, [3dc in corner st, W-st in each st to next corner st] 4 times, sl st in first dc made. End colour B.

Rnd 3: Repeat row 2 using colour C.

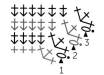

Base round

Whether you choose a sew-on or crochet-on edging pattern, always start by working a base round of double crochet around the afghan to provide a stable foundation (page 123). The base round is not included in the pattern instructions, but it is visible in the photographed crochet-on edgings and is shown in grey on the crochet-on edging charts.

Curvy

A

B

Base round

KEY

○ ch

• sl st

+ dc

⋊⋉ dc3tog

┬ tr

◄ begin round

- **Hook:** 5mm
- **Yarn:** DK
- **Multiple:** 4 + 3 + 4 corner sts
- **Technique:** Crochet-on (page 122)

Special stitch

Double crochet 3 together (dc3tog): Work dc in each of next 3 sts but omit final yo of each dc, yo and pull through all 4 loops on hook.

Pattern

Rnd 1: Join colour A in 2nd dc of any corner 3dc of base round, ch3 (counts as 1 tr), 6tr in same place, skip 1 st, dc in next st, *[skip 1 st, 5tr in next st, skip 1 st, dc in next st] to 1 st before next corner st, skip 1 st**, 7tr in corner st; rep from * twice more, then from * to ** once, sl st in top of beg ch3. End colour A.

Rnd 2: Join colour B in next st, ch1 and dc in same place, dc in next st, *3dc in next st, dc in next 2 sts, dc3tog in next 3 sts, [dc in next st, 3dc in next dc, dc in next st, dc3tog in next 3 sts] to 2nd tr of next corner**, dc in next 2 sts; rep from * twice more, then from * to ** once, sl st in first dc made. End colour B.

Note

All of the photographs show the edgings as if they were hanging down from the bottom of an afghan. The charts are drawn to match the orientation of each edging as you are making it.

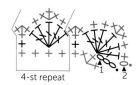

4-st repeat

Spikes

A

KEY

o ch	$\top$ tr
• sl st	
+ dc	← direction of work
◄ begin row	

- **Hook:** 5mm
- **Yarn:** DK
- **Technique:** Sew-on (page 123)

Pattern

Row 1: Ch7, 4tr in 7th ch from hook, ch3, turn, sl st in 2nd ch from hook and next ch, dc in next 4 sts, ch1, skip 1 ch, dc in next ch, turn.

Row 2: Ch4 (counts as 1 tr, ch1), 4tr in ch1sp, ch3, turn, sl st in 2nd ch from hook and next ch, dc in next 4 sts, ch1, skip 1 ch, dc in next ch, turn.

Repeat row 2 until edging is the desired length.

Crab

A

Base round

KEY

o ch	$\widetilde{+}$ CS
• sl st	◄ begin round
+ dc	

- **Hook:** 5mm
- **Yarn:** DK
- **Multiple:** Any number of sts
- **Technique:** Crochet-on (page 122)

Special stitch

Crab stitch (CS) – reverse double crochet: Insert hook in next st to right of hook, yo and draw up a loop, yo and pull through both loops on hook.

Pattern

Rnd 1: Join colour A in 2nd dc of any corner 3dc of base round, ch1 and CS in same place, CS in each st of base round, sl st in first CS made. End colour A.

Arches

A

KEY

o ch	$\top$ tr
• sl st	← direction of work
+ dc	
◄ begin row	

- **Hook:** 5mm
- **Yarn:** DK
- **Technique:** Sew-on (page 123)

Pattern

Row 1: Ch6, (2tr, ch2, 2tr) in 4th ch from hook, skip 1 ch, tr in last ch, turn.

Row 2: Ch3 (counts as 1 tr), skip 2 sts, (2tr, ch2, 2tr) in ch2sp, ch5, sl st in first tr of last row, turn, ch1, 10dc in ch5sp just made, skip 2 sts, (2tr, ch2, 2tr) in ch2sp, skip 2 sts, tr in next st.

Repeat row 2 until edging is the desired length.

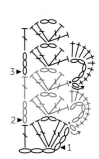

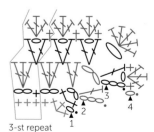

Mosaic

	A		E
	B		F
	C		G and base round
	D		

KEY

○ ch

• sl st

+ dc

◄ begin round

- **Hook:** 5mm
- **Yarn:** DK
- **Multiple:** 2 + 1 + 4 corner sts
- **Technique:** Crochet-on (page 122)

Pattern

Rnd 1: Join colour A in 2nd dc of any corner 3dc of base round, ch1 *(dc, ch2, dc) in corner st, ch1, skip 1 st, [dc in next st, ch1, skip 1 st] to next corner st; rep from * 3 times more, sl st in first dc made. End colour A.

Rnd 2: Join colour B in corner ch2sp, ch1, *(dc, ch2, dc) in ch2sp, ch1, skip 1 st, [dc in next ch1sp, ch1, skip 1 st] to next corner ch2sp; rep from * 3 times more, sl st in first dc made. End colour B.

Rnd 3: Repeat round 2 using colour C.

Rnd 4: Repeat round 2 using colour D.

Rnd 5: Repeat round 2 using colour E.

Rnd 6: Repeat round 2 using colour F.

Rnd 7: Repeat round 2 using colour G.

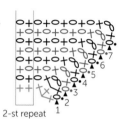

2-st repeat

Fancy

	A
	B
	C
	D
	Base round

KEY

○ ch

• sl st

+ dc

T tr

V V-st

◄ begin round

- **Hook:** 5mm
- **Yarn:** DK
- **Multiple:** 3 + 2 + 4 corner sts
- **Technique:** Crochet-on (page 122)

Special stitch

V-stitch (V-st): [Tr, ch1, tr] in place indicated.

Pattern

Rnd 1: Join colour A in 2nd dc of any corner 3dc of base round, ch1, *(dc, ch2, dc) in corner st, ch2, skip 2 sts, [dc in next st, ch2, skip 2 sts] to next corner st; rep from * 3 times more, sl st in first dc made. End colour A.

Rnd 2: Join colour B in corner ch2sp, ch3 (counts as 1 tr), (tr, ch2, 2tr) in same place, *[skip 1 st, 3tr in ch2sp] to next corner ch2sp**, (2tr, ch2, 2tr) in corner ch2sp; rep from * twice more, then from * to ** once, sl st in top of beg ch3. End colour B.

Rnd 3: Join colour C in corner ch2sp, ch4 (counts as 1 tr, ch1), ([tr, ch1] twice, tr) in same place, *[V-st in gap between next 2 groups of tr] to next corner ch2sp**, (V-st, ch1, V-st) in corner ch2sp; rep from * twice more, then from * to ** once, sl st in 3rd ch of beg ch4. End colour C.

Rnd 4: Join colour D, ch1, dc in first st, *3tr in ch1sp, dc in next st, 5tr in corner ch1sp, dc in next st, 3tr in ch1sp, [dc between next 2 sts, 3tr in ch1sp] to last V-st before corner ch1sp**, dc between next 2 sts; rep from * twice more, then from* to ** once, sl st in first dc made. End colour D.

3-st repeat

Skill level: 2

Flounce

A
B
C
Base round

KEY

○	ch	◀	begin round
•	sl st	←	turn work
+	dc		

 V-st

 bobble

- **Hook:** 5mm
- **Yarn:** DK
- **Multiple:** 2 + 1 + 4 corner sts
- **Technique:** Crochet-on (page 122)

Special stitches

V-stitch (V-st): [Tr, ch1, tr] in place indicated.

Bobble (BO): Work 5tr in place indicated but omit final yo of each tr, yo and pull through all 6 loops on hook.

Pattern

Rnd 1: Join colour A in 2nd dc of any corner 3dc of base round, ch1, *(dc, ch2, dc) in corner st, ch1, skip 1 st, [dc in next st, ch1, skip 1 st] to next corner st; rep from * 3 times more, sl st in first dc made. End colour A.

Rnd 2: Join colour B in ch2sp, ch4 (counts as 1 tr, ch1), (tr, ch2, tr, ch1, tr) in same place, *[skip 1 st, V-st in ch1sp] to next corner ch2sp**, (V-st, ch2, V-st) in ch2sp; rep from * twice more, then from * to ** once, sl st in 3rd ch of beg ch4. End colour B. Turn.

Rnd 3: Join colour C, ch1, dc in first st, *BO in ch1sp, dc in next st, BO in corner ch2sp, dc in next st, BO in ch1sp, [dc between next 2 sts, BO in ch1sp] to last V-st before corner ch2sp**, dc between next 2 sts; rep from * twice more, then from * to ** once, sl st in first dc made. End colour C.

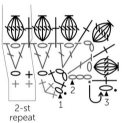

2-st repeat

Skill level: 2

Flowery

A

KEY

○	ch
•	sl st
⊤	tr

 CL

◀ begin row

← direction of work

- **Hook:** 5mm
- **Yarn:** DK
- **Technique:** Sew-on (page 123)

Special stitch

Cluster (CL): Work 3tr in place indicated but omit final yo of each tr, yo and pull through all 4 loops on hook.

Pattern

Row 1: Ch9, tr in 7th ch from hook (first ch4 counts as 1 tr, ch1), tr in next ch, 2tr in last ch, ch9, sl st in 5th ch from hook, turn, [ch2, CL, ch2, sl st] 3 times in ring, ch5, skip 1 tr, tr in next 3 sts, ch1, skip 1 ch, tr in next ch, turn.

Row 2: Ch4 (counts as 1 tr, ch1), skip 1 ch, tr in next 2 sts, 2tr in next st, ch9, sl st in 5th ch from hook, turn, [ch2, CL, ch2, sl st] 3 times in ring, ch5, skip 1 tr, tr in next 3 sts, ch1, skip 1 ch, tr in next ch, turn.

Repeat row 2 until edging is the desired length.

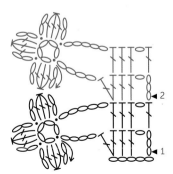

Ruffled

A
B
C
D
Base round

KEY

○ ch

• sl st

+ dc

‡ BPdc

⊤ tr

〇 Puff

beg CL

CL

◄ begin round

- **Hook:** 5mm
- **Yarn:** DK
- **Multiple:** 6 + 5 + 4 corner sts
- **Technique:** Crochet-on (page 122)

Special stitches

Puff stitch (Puff): [Yo, insert hook in place indicated, yo and draw up a loop] twice, yo and pull through all 5 loops on hook.

Beginning cluster (beg CL): Ch2, work 2tr in place indicated but omit final yo of each tr, yo and pull through all 3 loops on hook.

Cluster (CL): Work 3tr in place indicated but omit final yo of each tr, yo and pull through all 4 loops on hook.

Pattern

Rnd 1: Join colour A in 2nd dc of any corner 3dc of base round, ch3 (counts as 1 tr), 11tr in same place, skip 2 sts, dc in next st, *[skip 2 sts, 8tr in next st, skip 2 sts, dc in next st] to 2 sts before next corner st, skip 2 sts**, 12tr in corner st; rep from * twice more, then from * to ** once, sl st in top of beg ch3. End colour A.

Rnd 2: Join colour B, ch2 (does not count as a st), *skip 1 st, [Puff in next st, ch1] 9 times, Puff in next st, skip 1 st, BPdc in next st, [skip 1 st, (Puff in next st, ch1) 5 times, Puff in next st, skip 1 st, BPdc in next st] to next corner 12tr; rep from * 3 times more, sl st in top of first Puff made. End colour B.

Rnd 3: Join colour C in next ch1sp, beg CL in same place, ch2, [CL in next ch1sp, ch2] 7 times, CL in next ch1sp, skip next Puff, BPdc in next st, *skip next Puff, [CL in next ch1sp, ch2] 4 times, CL in next ch1sp, skip next Puff, BPdc in next st] to next corner 10 Puffs**, skip next Puff, [CL in next ch1sp, ch2] 8 times, CL in next ch1sp, skip next Puff, BPdc in next st; rep from * twice more, then from * to ** once, sl st in top of beg CL. End colour C.

Rnd 4: Join colour D in top of beg CL, ch1, *[3dc in ch2sp, ch4, sl st in 2nd ch from hook and next 2 ch] 7 times, 3dc in next ch2sp, skip next CL, BPdc in next st, [(3dc in ch2sp, ch4, sl st in 2nd ch from hook and next 2 ch) 3 times, 3dc in next ch2sp, skip next CL, BPdc in next st] to next corner 9CL; rep from * 3 times more, sl st in first dc made. End colour D.

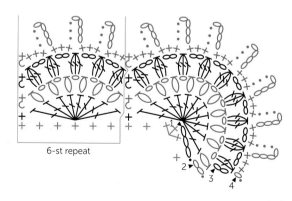

6-st repeat

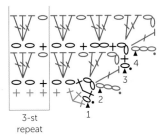

Skill level: 1

Granny

A
B
C
Base round

KEY

◯ ch

• sl st

+ dc

🕈 tr

◀ begin round

■ **Hook:** 5mm
■ **Yarn:** DK
■ **Multiple:** 3 + 2 + 4 corner sts
■ **Technique:** Crochet-on (page 122)

Pattern

Rnd 1: Join colour A in 2nd dc of any corner 3dc of base round, ch1, *(dc, ch2, dc) in corner st, ch2, skip 2 sts, [dc in next st, ch2, skip 2 sts] to next corner st; rep from * 3 times more, sl st in first dc made. End colour A.

Rnd 2: Join colour B in corner ch2sp, ch3 (counts as 1 tr), (tr, ch2, 2tr) in same place, *[ch1, skip 1 st, 3tr in ch2sp] to next corner ch2sp, ch1, skip 1 st**, (2tr, ch2, 2tr) in corner ch2sp; rep from * twice more, then from * to ** once,

sl st in top of beg ch3. End colour B.

Rnd 3: Join colour A in corner ch2sp, ch1, *(dc, ch2, dc) in corner ch2sp, ch2, skip 2 sts, [dc in ch1sp, ch2, skip next tr group] to next corner ch2sp; rep from * 3 times more, sl st in first dc made. End colour A.

Rnd 4: Repeat row 2 using colour C.

3-st repeat

Skill level: 2

Prism

A
B
C
D
Base round

KEY

◯ ch

• sl st

+ dc

🕈 tr

🕸 PC

◀ begin round

■ **Hook:** 5mm
■ **Yarn:** DK
■ **Multiple:** 10 + 1 + 4 corner sts
■ **Technique:** Crochet-on (page 122)

Special stitch

Popcorn (PC): Work 5tr in place indicated, remove hook from loop, insert hook from front to back in top of first tr, pick up dropped loop and pull through loop on hook.

Pattern

Rnd 1: Join colour A in 2nd dc of any corner 3dc of base round, ch3 (counts as 1 tr), 2tr in same place, *tr in next st, [ch1, skip 1 st, (PC in next st, ch1, skip 1 st) 4 times, tr in next st] to next corner st, 3tr in corner st; rep from * 3 times more, sl st in top of beg ch3. End colour A.

Rnd 2: Join colour B in next corner st, ch3 (counts as 1 tr), 2tr in same place,

*ch1, skip 1 st, tr in next st, [tr in ch1sp, ch1, (skip PC, PC in ch1sp, ch1) 3 times, skip PC, tr in ch1sp, tr in next st] to last ch1sp before next corner st, ch1, skip 1 st**, 3tr in corner st; rep from * twice more, then from * to ** once, sl st in top of beg ch3. End colour B.

Rnd 3: Join colour C in next corner st, ch3 (counts as 1 tr), 2tr in same place, *ch1, skip 1 st, tr in ch1sp, tr in next st, [tr in next st, tr in ch1sp, ch1, (skip PC, PC in ch1sp, ch1) twice, skip PC, tr in ch1sp, tr in next 2 sts] to 2 sts and 1 chsp before next corner st, tr in ch1sp, ch1, skip 1 st**, 3tr in corner st; rep from * twice more, then from * to ** once, sl st in top of beg ch3. End colour C.

Rnd 4: Join colour D in next corner st, ch3 (counts as 1 tr), 2tr in same place, *ch1, skip 1 st, tr in ch1sp, tr in next 2 sts, [tr in next 2 sts, tr in ch1sp, ch1, skip PC,

PC in ch1sp, ch1, skip PC, tr in ch1sp, tr in next 3 sts) to last (tr, ch1sp, tr) before next corner st, tr in next st, tr in ch1sp, ch1, skip 1 st**, 3tr in corner st; rep from * twice more, then from * to ** once, sl st in top of beg ch3. End colour D.

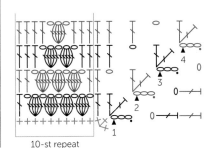

10-st repeat

Techniques

Use this section to help brush up your skills or as an introductory guide if you are new to crochet. You will find plenty of practical advice and information on working the basic stitches and variations, guidance on how to read crochet patterns and follow charts, plus advice on joining blocks together and adding an edging to your afghan.

Materials and Notions

When you walk into a yarn shop, you'll find yourself bombarded with gorgeous yarns in scrumptious colours, differing weights and all types of textures. The choice is exciting but can be a little perplexing, and the same is true for hooks and accessories. Use this guide to find out what you need to get started.

Yarn choice

Suitable yarns for crochet range from very fine cotton to chunky wool. As a general rule, yarns that have a smooth texture and a medium or high twist are the easiest to work with. For making afghans, a medium-weight yarn is probably best, as it works up quickly, has good drape and stitch definition, and provides a warm and cosy blanket. All of the patterns in this book have been worked in DK yarn.

Another thing to consider while standing in front of all that yarn is the fibre content and the kind of drape that you would like to achieve in your project. Before purchasing enough yarn to complete a project, it's a good idea to buy just one ball. Make a test swatch, wash it following the instructions on the ball band, block it to shape and see whether you are comfortable using the yarn and whether it turns out how you'd intended.

Yarn fibres

Yarns come in a range of different fibres and fibre combinations.

Wool

Wool is an excellent choice for afghans. It is a resilient fibre that feels good to crochet with and has great stitch definition. If you are making a project that you would like to hand down to future generations and it is within your budget, wool is the fibre to use. Do find out whether or not the wool can be machine-washed.

Acrylic

Acrylic yarn is a perfect choice for beginners and popular with crochet enthusiasts. It's great for practising stitches and techniques and testing colour combinations. Acrylic yarns come in a huge array of colours and it is an affordable choice for your first project. Although acrylic can pill and lose its shape eventually, it does have the benefit of being machine-washable, making it a good choice for items that may require frequent washing.

Combination yarns

A yarn comprised of both wool and synthetic fibre is a dependable choice. Picking something that has a small percentage of synthetic fibre (for example, nylon or acrylic) makes a nice yarn to work with and launder, while still retaining the advantages of wool.

Cotton and cotton mixes

Cotton can present more of a challenge for beginners. It can be a little stiff to work with, but the stitches are crisp and neat. A cotton mix is usually softer to work with, yet still retains crisp, neat stitch definition. Afghans crocheted with cotton or a cotton mix are durable and cool, so are perfect for summer.

Novelty yarns

Although novelty yarns are tactile and enticing, they are not easy to work with. You can use a splash of novelty yarn to add some interest, but on the whole they are tricky to use and also hide the stitches.

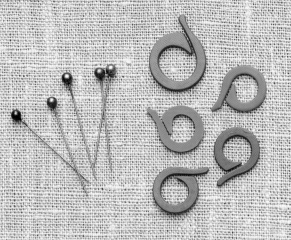

Crochet hooks

Hooks come in different sizes and materials. The material a hook is made from can affect your tension. To start out, it's best to use aluminium hooks, as they have a pointed head and well-defined throat and work well with most yarns. Bamboo hooks are also pleasing to work with, but can be slippery with some yarns. Plastic hooks can be squeaky with synthetic yarns. You can also purchase hooks with soft-grip or wooden handles, which are great to work with, particularly if crochet becomes an obsession.

What size hook?

You may find that using the hook size recommended for a particular yarn or pattern isn't satisfactory, and your work may be too tight or too loose. Try different hook sizes until you are happy with the completed swatch. Ultimately, you want to use a hook and yarn weight that you are comfortable with – yarn/hook recommendations are not set in stone. Be aware that not all yarn labels give a recommended hook size. Use the recommended knitting needle size as a guide, or a hook one or two sizes bigger.

Notions

Although all you need to get started is a hook and some yarn, it's handy to have the following items in your work bag.

Scissors

Use a pair of small, sharp embroidery scissors.

Ruler and measuring tape

A rigid ruler is best for measuring tension. A sturdy measuring tape is good for taking larger measurements.

Stitch markers

Split-ring markers are handy for keeping track of the first stitch of a row, particularly when starting out. Also use them to hold the working loop when you put your work down for the night.

Pins

Use rustproof, glass-headed pins for wet and steam blocking.

Needles

Yarn or tapestry needles are used for sewing seams and weaving in yarn ends. Choose needles with blunt ends to avoid splitting stitches. Yarn needles have different-sized eyes, so choose one that will accommodate the weight of yarn you will be using.

Starting and Finishing

Crochet can be worked in rows, beginning with a foundation chain, or in rounds, working outwards from a foundation ring of chain stitches or a magic ring. See page 116 for a reminder of how to work the basic crochet stitches.

Holding the hook and yarn

The most common way of holding the hook is shown here, but if this doesn't feel comfortable to you, try grasping the flat section of the hook between your thumb and forefinger as if you were holding a knife.

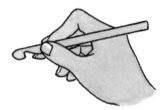

1 Holding the hook like a pen is the most widely used method. Centre the tips of your right thumb and forefinger over the flat section of the hook.

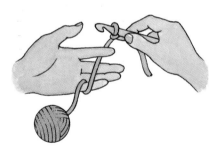

2 To control the supply and keep an even tension on the yarn, loop the short end of the yarn over your left forefinger, and take the yarn coming from the ball loosely around the little finger on the same hand. Use the middle finger on the same hand to help hold the work. If you are left-handed, hold the hook in your left hand and the yarn in your right.

Making a slip knot

1 Loop the yarn as shown, insert the hook into the loop, catch the yarn with the hook and pull it through to make a loop over the hook.

2 Gently pull the yarn to tighten the loop around the hook and complete the slip knot.

Foundation chain

The pattern will tell you how many chains to make. This may be a specific number or a multiple. If a pattern tells you to make a multiple of 3 + 2, this does not mean make a multiple of 5. It means that you should make a multiple of 3 and then add 2 chains – eg, 3 + 2, 6 + 2, 9 + 2 and so on. You may also be instructed to add a turning chain for the first row.

1 Holding the hook with the slip knot in your right hand and the yarn in your left hand, wrap the yarn over the hook. Draw the yarn through to make a new loop and complete the first chain stitch.

2 Repeat this process, drawing a new loop of yarn through the loop already on the hook until the foundation chain is the required length. Count each V-shaped loop on the front of the chain as one chain stitch, except for the loop on the hook, which is not counted. If your chain stitches are tight, try using a larger hook for the foundation chain. After every few stitches, move up the thumb and finger that are grasping the chain to keep the chain stitches even.

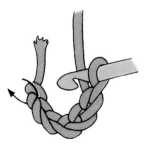

Foundation ring

1 Work a short length of foundation chain as specified in the pattern. Join the chains into a ring by working a slip stitch into the first chain of the foundation chain.

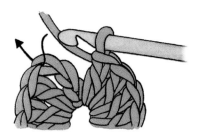

2 Work the first round of stitches into the centre of the ring unless specified otherwise. At the end of the round, the final stitch is usually joined to the first stitch with a slip stitch.

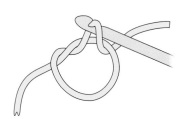

Magic ring

Use this alternative to a foundation ring for working in the round when you want to avoid a hole in the centre of your work. Wrap the yarn into a ring, insert the hook and draw a loop through. Work the first round of crochet stitches into this ring, then pull the yarn tail tightly to close the ring.

Turning and starting chains

When working crochet, you will need to work a specific number of extra chains at the beginning of each row or round. When the work is turned at the end of a straight row, the extra chains are called a turning chain, and when they are worked at the beginning of a round, they are called a starting chain.

The extra chains bring the hook up to the correct height for the stitch you will be working next. The turning or starting chain is counted as the first stitch of the row or round, except when working double crochet where the single turning chain is ignored. A chain may be longer than the number required for the stitch, and in that case counts as one stitch plus a number of chains.

At the end of the row, the final stitch is usually worked into the turning chain at the beginning of the previous row. The final stitch may be worked into the top chain of the turning chain or into another specified stitch of the chain. At the end of a round, the final stitch is usually joined to the starting chain with a slip stitch.

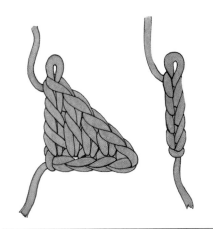

Number of turning chains

- **Double crochet (dc):** 1 turning chain
- **Half treble crochet (htr):** 2 turning chains
- **Treble crochet (tr):** 3 turning chains
- **Double treble crochet (dtr):** 4 turning chains
- **Triple treble crochet (trtr):** 5 turning chains
- **Quadruple treble crochet (qtr):** 6 turning chains

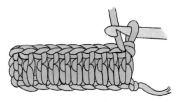

Fastening off

When you have completed your crochet, cut the yarn about 15cm (6in) from the last stitch. Wrap the yarn over the hook and draw the yarn end through the loop on the hook. Gently pull the yarn to tighten the last stitch, then weave in the yarn end.

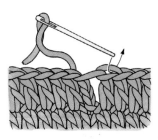

Finishing the last round

For a neater finish, don't use a slip stitch to join the last stitch of the final round to the first stitch of the round. Instead, fasten off the yarn after the last stitch, thread a yarn needle with the end of yarn and pass it under the top loops of the first stitch of the round and back through the centre of the last stitch.

Weaving in ends

At the end of making your project, you will need to weave in any yarn ends from changing colours and sewing seams. For crochet worked in rows, use a yarn needle to sew in ends diagonally on the wrong side. For crochet worked in rounds, sew in ends under stitches for a few centimetres. If the pattern doesn't allow this, sew under a few stitches, then up through the back of a stitch, and under a few more stitches on the next row.

Basic Stitches

All crochet stitches are based on a loop pulled through another loop by a hook. There are only a few stitches to master, each of a different length. Here is a concise guide to the basic stitches used to make the afghans.

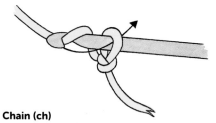

Chain (ch)
Wrap the yarn over the hook and pull it through the loop on the hook to form a new loop on the hook.

Extended double crochet (Ext dc)
Insert the hook into the specified stitch, yarn over hook and pull it through the stitch (2 loops on hook). Chain 1. Yarn over hook and pull it through both loops.

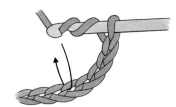

Double treble crochet (dtr)
Yarn over hook twice, insert the hook into the specified stitch, yarn over hook and pull it through the stitch (4 loops on hook). *Yarn over hook and pull it through two loops; repeat from * twice more.

Slip stitch (sl st)
Insert the hook into the specified stitch, wrap the yarn over the hook and pull it through the stitch and the loop on the hook.

Half treble crochet (htr)
Yarn over hook, insert the hook into the specified stitch, yarn over hook and pull it through the stitch (3 loops on hook). Yarn over hook and pull it through all three loops.

Double crochet (dc)
Insert the hook into the specified stitch, wrap the yarn over the hook and pull it through the stitch (2 loops on hook). Yarn over hook and pull it through both loops.

Treble crochet (tr)
Yarn over hook, insert the hook into the specified stitch, yarn over hook and pull it through the stitch (3 loops on hook). *Yarn over hook and pull it through two loops; repeat from * once more.

Making taller stitches

You can make taller stitches by wrapping the yarn over the hook as many times as you wish before inserting the hook into the specified stitch. For example, wrap the yarn over the hook three times to make a triple treble crochet (trtr). Make four wraps for a quadruple treble crochet (qtr) and so on. Complete the stitch in the same way as double treble crochet, working off two loops at a time in the usual way.

Simple Stitch Variations

Basic stitches may be varied in many ways to achieve different effects. These simple variations are all made by inserting the hook in different places in the crochet to work the stitches.

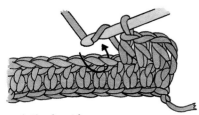

Through the front loop
Rather than inserting the hook under both top loops to work the next stitch in the usual way, insert it only under the front loop.

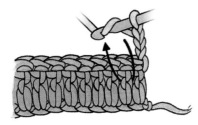

Around the front post (FP)
Work around the stem of the stitch, inserting the hook from front to back, around the post and to the front again.

Into a row below (spike stitch)
Spike stitches are made by inserting the hook one or more rows below the previous row. To work a double crochet spike stitch, for example, insert the hook as directed by the pattern, wrap the yarn over the hook and draw it through, lengthen the loop to the height of the working row, then complete the stitch.

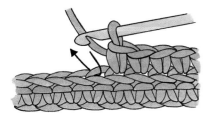

Through the back loop
Rather than inserting the hook under both top loops to work the next stitch in the usual way, insert it only under the back loop.

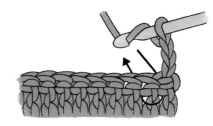

Around the back post (BP)
Work around the stem of the stitch, inserting the hook from back to front, around the post and to the back again.

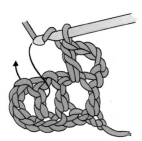

Into a chain space (chsp)
Insert the hook into the space below a chain or chains. Here, a dtr is being worked into a ch1sp.

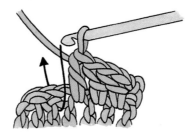

Into a stitch space
Insert the hook between the stitches of the previous row, instead of into a stitch itself.

Into the 'V' (waistcoat stitch – W-st)
This variation is worked into the right side of a double crochet stitch. Instead of inserting the hook under the top two loops of the stitch, this time insert it into the 'V' formed by the two vertical strands at the front of the stitch.

There should be three strands of yarn above the hook when you do this, two from the top of the stitch and one from the back of the stitch. Complete the double crochet in the usual way.

Special Stitches

By working multiple stitches in the same place or working several stitches together at the top, or a combination of both, you can create interesting shapes, patterns and textures. The turning or starting chain may be counted as the first stitch of a cluster, bobble, popcorn or puff stitch.

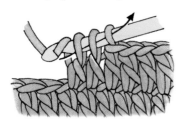

Decrease (eg, dc2tog, tr3tog)
One or two stitches can be decreased by working two or three incomplete stitches together. Work the specified number of stitches, omitting the final stage (the last yarn over) of each stitch so that the last loop of each stitch remains on the hook. Wrap the yarn over the hook and draw it through all of the loops on the hook. The method is the same for all the basic crochet stitches.

Cluster (CL)
A cluster can be made from a multiple of any of the basic crochet stitches. Work the specified number of stitches in the places indicated in the pattern, omitting the final stage of each stitch so that the last loop of each stitch remains on the hook. Wrap the yarn over the hook and draw it through all of the loops on the hook.

Popcorn (PC)
A popcorn is a group of treble crochet or longer stitches worked in the same place and then folded and closed at the top so that the popcorn is raised from the background stitches. Work the specified number of stitches in the same place. Take the hook out of the working loop and insert it under both top loops of the first stitch of the popcorn. Pick up the working loop with the hook and draw it through to fold the group of stitches and close the popcorn at the top.

Increase (eg, 5tr in next ch)
This technique is used to increase the total number of stitches when shaping an item, or to create a decorative effect such as a shell. Simply work the required number of stitches in the same place. Increases may be worked at the edges of flat pieces, or at any point along a row or round.

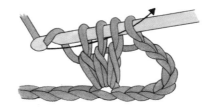

Bobble (BO)
A bobble is a group of between three and six treble crochet or longer stitches worked in the same place and closed at the top. Work the specified number of stitches, omitting the final stage of each stitch so that the last loop of each stitch remains on the hook. Wrap the yarn over the hook and draw it through all of the loops on the hook.

Puff stitch
A puff stitch is a cluster of half treble crochet stitches worked in the same place. Work the specified number of stitches, omitting the final stage of each stitch so that two loops of each one remain on the hook. Wrap the yarn over hook and draw it through all of the loops on the hook.

Colourwork

Most of the afghan patterns use a single colour for each row or round, with the new colour being joined at the end of a row or round. Tapestry and intarsia designs involve using multiple colours across the row. In tapestry crochet, the unworked colour is carried behind the row and woven in. Intarsia crochet features large and sometimes irregularly shaped sections of different colours, and each section is worked with a separate ball of yarn.

Changing colour on a row

When working the last stitch of the old colour, omit the final stage (the last yarn over) to leave the stitch incomplete. Wrap the new yarn over the hook and draw it through all of the loops on the hook to complete the stitch. The new yarn will form the top loops of the next stitch in the new colour.

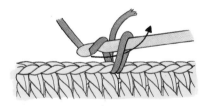

Changing colour on a round

Method 1: When joining the last stitch of the round to the first stitch using a slip stitch, work the joining slip stitch using the new colour. Method 2 (above): Insert the hook where required and draw up a loop of the new colour, leaving a 10cm (4in) tail. Work the specified number of starting chains. Continue with the new yarn.

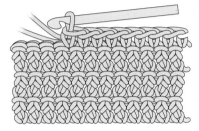

Tapestry crochet

1 Change to the new colour (pink) in the usual way. Continue following the pattern, carrying the unused yarn (blue) along the top of the previous row at the back of the work and crocheting over it. After the next colour change, continue to carry and work over the unused yarn in the same way.

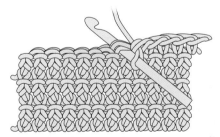

2 On the next and all other rows, insert the hook under the carried yarn and into the stitch to lock the carried yarn in place.

Intarsia crochet

Use a separate ball or bobbin of yarn for each area of colour. If the same colour is used twice across the row, you will need two separate balls of it.

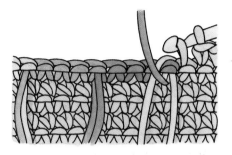

1 Follow the pattern, changing colours where indicated in the usual way and dropping the unused yarns to the wrong side of the work. At each colour change on subsequent rows, make sure that you loop the new yarn around the old one on the wrong side of the work to prevent holes.

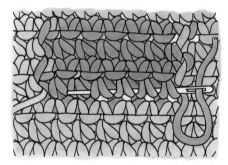

2 Take extra care when dealing with all the yarn ends on a piece of intarsia. Carefully weave each end into an area of crochet worked in the same colour so that it will not be visible on the right side.

Reading Patterns and Charts

With all those symbols, abbreviations and charts, crochet can seem daunting and complex to begin with. A little explanation, though, and all becomes clear.

Abbreviations are used to make crochet patterns quicker and easier to follow. Abbreviations and chart symbols may vary from one pattern publisher to another, so always check that you understand the system in use before commencing work. Some patterns use special abbreviations and symbols and specific stitch instructions, and these are explained with each pattern.

Understanding symbols

Symbol	Meaning
*	Start of repeat
**	End of last repeat
[ ]	Repeat the instructions within the brackets the stated number of times
( )	Can either be explanatory (counts as 1 tr) or can be read as a group of stitches worked in the same place (tr, ch2, tr)
►	An arrowhead indicates the beginning of a row or round

Symbols joined at top

 A group of symbols joined at the top should be worked together at the top, as in cluster stitches and for decreasing (eg, dc2tog, tr3tog)

Symbols joined at base

 Symbols joined at the base should all be worked into the same stitch below

Symbols joined at top and base

 Sometimes a group of stitches are joined at both top and bottom, making a puff, bobble or popcorn

Symbols on a curve

 Sometimes symbols are drawn at an angle, depending on the construction of the stitch pattern

Distorted symbols

 Some symbols may be lengthened, curved or spiked, to indicate where the hook is inserted below

Symbols and abbreviations

Symbol	Meaning	Abbreviation
○	Chain	ch
•	Slip stitch	sl st
+	Double crochet	dc
T	Half treble crochet	htr
‡	Treble crochet	tr
‡	Double treble crochet	dtr
‡	Triple treble crochet	trtr
‡	Quadruple treble crochet	qtr
eg, cluster of 3tr	Cluster	CL
eg, bobble of 5tr	Bobble	BO
eg, puff of 5htr	Puff stitch	Puff
eg, popcorn of 5tr	Popcorn	PC
eg, dc through back loop	Through back loop	–
eg, htr through front loop	Through front loop	–
⌡	Back post	BP
⌠	Front post	FP
–	Beginning	beg
–	Chain space	chsp
–	Repeat	rep
–	Right side / Wrong side	RS / WS
–	Stitch(es)	st(s)
–	Together	tog
–	Yarn over	yo

Reading charts

Each design in this book is accompanied by a chart, which should be read together with the written instructions. Once you are used to the symbols, they are quick and easy to follow. All charts are read from the right side.

Charts in rows
- Right-side rows start at the right, and are read from right to left.
- Wrong-side rows start at the left, and are read from left to right.
- The beginning of each row is indicated by an arrow.

Charts in rounds
These charts begin at the centre, and each round is read anticlockwise, in the same direction as working. The beginning of each round is indicated by an arrow. Some charts have been stretched to show all the stitches.

Calculating yarn amounts

Each of the block patterns in this book provides the amount of yarn required to make one block. Multiply this amount by the number of blocks you plan to make and round up to the nearest metre or yard. On page 124, you will find yarn quantities for three sizes of afghan for all 40 patterns. These quantities are approximate and based on using DK yarn and the size of hook recommended for the pattern.

The best way to calculate how much yarn you will need is to make a few blocks or work a few repeats of a pattern in the yarn and colour combination you intend to use, then unravel them. Measure the amount of yarn used for each colour, take the average length and multiply by the number of blocks or pattern repeats you intend to make. Add extra yarn for joining blocks and working edgings.

Tension and Blocking

It's important to crochet a test swatch before you start your project to establish tension. To finish your afghan neatly, you will need to block it. You can use the tension swatch to test blocking and cleaning methods.

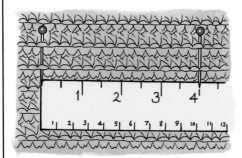

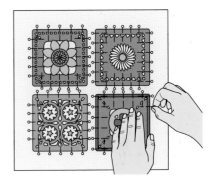

Measuring tension

No two people will crochet to the exact same tension, even when working with identical yarn and hooks. Always make a test swatch before starting a project so that you can compare your tension with the pattern tension and get an idea of how the finished project will feel and drape. It's also useful for testing out different colour combinations.

To test your tension, make a sample swatch in the yarn you intend to use following the pattern directions. Block the sample and then measure again. If your swatch is larger, try making another using a smaller hook. If your swatch is smaller, try making another using a bigger hook. Also do this if the fabric feels too loose and floppy or too dense and rigid. Keep trying until you find a hook size that will give you the required tension, or until you are happy with the drape and feel of your work. Ultimately, it's more important that you use a hook and yarn you are comfortable with than that you rigidly follow the pattern instructions.

Blocking

Blocking is crucial to set the stitches and even out the piece. Choose a method based on the care label of the yarn. When in doubt, use the wet method. Use an ironing board or old quilt, or make a blocking board by securing one or two layers of quilter's wadding, covered with a sheet of cotton fabric, over a flat board.

Wet method – acrylic and wool/acrylic mix
Using rustproof pins, pin the crochet fabric to the correct measurements on a flat surface and dampen using a spray bottle of cold water. Pat the fabric to help the moisture penetrate. Ease stitches into position, keeping rows and stitches straight. Allow to dry before removing the pins.

Steam method – wools and cottons
Pin out the fabric as above. For fabric with raised stitches, pin it right side up to avoid squashing the stitches; otherwise, pin it wrong side up. Steam lightly, holding the iron 2.5cm (1in) above the fabric. Allow the steam to penetrate for several seconds. It is safer to avoid pressing, but if you choose to do so, cover with a clean towel or cloth first.

Joining and Edging

If you are making your afghan from a block pattern, you will need to sew or crochet the blocks together before adding an edging. A crochet edging does not just finish off a project with style, but it also helps the afghan to hold its shape and keeps the edges from stretching. See page 100 for a selection of edging patterns.

Joining blocks

Blocks can be joined by sewing or by crochet. Pin seams together to help match up the blocks and give a neat finish. Use the same yarn that you used for the blocks, or a finer yarn, preferably with the same fibre content.

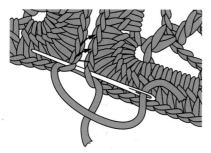

Oversewing
Using a yarn needle, sew through the back or front loops of corresponding stitches. For extra strength, work two stitches into the end loops.

Backstitch
Hold the blocks with right sides together. Using a yarn needle, work a line of backstitches along the edge.

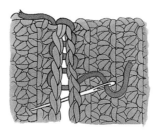

Mattress stitch
Lay the blocks wrong side up and with edges touching. Using a yarn needle, weave back and forth around the centres of the stitches, without pulling the stitches too tight.

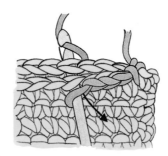

Crochet seams
Join the blocks with wrong sides together for a visible seam, or with right sides together for an invisible one. Work a row of slip stitch (above) or double crochet through both top loops of each block. When using this method along the side edges of blocks worked in rows, work enough evenly spaced stitches so that the seam is not too tight.

Crochet-on edgings

Calculate how many stitches the edging pattern needs, including corners. When working the base round (page 123), increase or decrease the number of stitches along each edge of the afghan to match the edging pattern you have chosen. Make sure increase or decrease stitches are evenly spaced to avoid puckering. Using markers to indicate where pattern repeats will lie will help you to visualise it.

Crochet-on edging calculations
Each edging pattern starts in the corner stitch of the base round and includes instructions for working the corners. Some designs require a specific multiple of stitches in order to work the pattern repeat. This is written in the pattern instructions as:

- Multiple: x + x + 4 corner sts

The corner stitches will be the second double crochet of each corner of the base round, so after working your base round you will have four corner stitches (1 st at each corner). If the pattern requires a multiple of 3 + 2 + 4 corner stitches, you should have a multiple of 3 stitches with 2 stitches remaining along each edge (eg, 3 + 2, 6 + 2, 9 + 2 and so on), plus 4 corner stitches. Count the stitches along each edge between the corner stitches to check you have the correct number. If you do not, you can work another base round, decreasing or adding stitches evenly as needed.

Sew-on edgings

Sew-on edgings are usually worked sideways by working a few stitches on each row for the length required. Make the edging longer than it appears to need to be. If possible, sew the edging in place as you make it, adding any extra length as you go.

Calculating how much you need
When calculating the amount you need, add about an extra 5–10cm (2–4in) of edging for every 100cm (40in) of afghan edge, allowing extra length to turn corners. Try out the edging on your tension swatch to help you calculate the correct number of stitches you will need for the edging to sit correctly around corners.

Attaching sew-on edgings

Don't fasten off the yarn in case you need to make adjustments to the length of the edging. Hold the working loop of the edging with a marker to keep it from unravelling. Place the edge of the afghan and the edge of the edging so that the right sides of both are facing you, with the edging on top. Pin in place and sew on the edging by oversewing through the front loops. Make any adjustments to the length of the edging, then fasten off the yarn and use the tail to join the two ends of the border together.

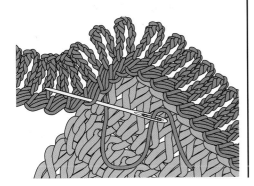

Base round

This is the most important step in working your edgings. A base round provides the edging with a good, stable foundation. It helps to even out untidy edges at row ends and any uneven stitches. Make the base round by crocheting one round of double crochet around the afghan, working three stitches in each corner. Work a base round for both crochet-on and sew-on edgings.

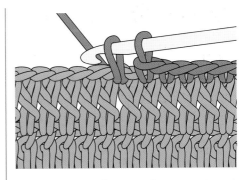

Across the top or bottom edge
When working across the top of a row, work 1dc into each stitch as you would if working another row. When working across the bottom edge of chain stitches, work 1dc in the remaining loop of each foundation chain.

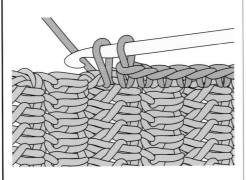

Along sides of row ends
When working on the side edge of an afghan worked in rows, insert the hook under two threads of the first (or last) stitch of each row. Place the stitches an even distance apart along the edge. Try a short length to test the number of stitches required for a flat result. As a guide:
- **Rows of dc:** 1dc in side edge of each row.
- **Rows of htr:** 3dc in side edge of every two rows.
- **Rows of tr:** 2dc in side edge of each row.
- **Rows of dtr:** 3dc in side edge of each row.

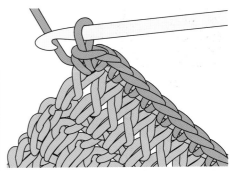

Around corners
You will need to add a couple of stitches at each corner to allow the base round to turn the corner without distorting the afghan. As a guide, corners are normally turned by working 3dc (or dc, htr, dc) into the corner. If you find the base round is too wavy or too taut after it has been completed, it will probably get worse once the rest of the edging has been worked. Take time at this point to pull out the base round and redo it using fewer stitches if the edge is too wavy, or using more stitches if the edge is too taut.

Yarn Quantities and Colours

Approximate yarn quantities are listed here for making three different sizes of afghan, excluding edgings. All block patterns should match these afghan sizes if you match the stated tension. For row-by-row patterns, the table also provides the length of foundation chain and number of whole repeats to work in order to match these afghan sizes as closely as possible. Adjust as necessary to suit your personal tension.

- **Baby blanket:** 90 x 90cm (36 x 36in); if using a square block pattern, make 36 blocks and join in 6 rows of 6 blocks.
- **Throw:** 150 x 180cm (60 x 72in); if using a square block pattern, make 120 blocks and join in 12 rows of 10 blocks.
- **Bedspread:** 210 x 225cm (84 x 90in); if using a square block pattern, make 210 blocks and join in 15 rows of 14 blocks.

- **Cascade colours:** All yarns are from Cascade Yarns' DK-weight 220 Superwash range. Please use the colour numbers provided as a guide only and be sure to check exact colours with your yarn supplier before purchasing.
- **Quantities:** Follow the advice on page 121 to calculate yarn amounts for other sizes or afghan and to double-check the quantities below using your chosen yarn and hook.

Pattern	Baby blanket	Throw	Bedspread	Cascade colours
Bobble Along p.10	Ch129; repeats = 62 wide x 5 high; A 44m (49yd), B 31m (34yd), C 142m (156yd), D 31m (34yd), E 86m (95yd), F 171m (188yd), G 117m (128yd), H 171m (188yd)	Ch213; repeats = 104 wide x 10 high; A 132m (145yd), B 94m (103yd), C 426m (466yd), D 94m (103yd), E 258m (283yd), F 515m (564yd), G 384yd (351m), H 515m (564yd)	Ch297; repeats = 146 wide x 12 high; A 222m (243yd), B 159m (174yd), C 721m (789yd), D 159m (174yd), E 436m (477yd), F 872m (954yd), G 594m (650yd), H 872m (954yd)	A 844, B 851, C 1942, D 871, E 837, F 839, G 824, H 827
Band of Hearts p.12	Ch83; repeats = 20 wide x 5 high; A 171m (188yd), B 45m (50yd), C 103m (113yd), D 256m (280yd), E 58m (64yd), F 86m (95yd), G 86m (95yd), H 92m (101yd)	Ch139; repeats = 34 wide x 10 high; A 577m (632yd), B 149m (163yd), C 346m (379yd), D 858m (939yd), E 198m (217yd), F 289m (317yd), G 289m (317yd), H 309m (338yd)	Ch191; repeats = 47 wide x 12 high; A 955m (1045yd), B 244m (267yd), C 571m (625yd), D 1416m (1549yd), E 328m (359yd), F 478m (523yd), G 478m (523yd), H 511m (559yd)	A 816, B 886, C 817, D 875, E 838, F 903, G 1942, H 879
Baby Diamonds p.14	Ch122; repeats = 10 wide x 8 high; A 297m (325yd), B 288m (315yd), C 293m (321yd), D 288m (315yd)	Ch206; repeats = 17 wide x 16 high; A 995m (1089yd), B 980m (1072yd), C 989m (1082yd), D 980m (1072yd)	Ch290; repeats = 24 wide x 21 high; A 1836m (2008yd), B 1815m (1985yd), C 1827m (1999yd), D 1815m (1985yd)	A 847, B 836, C 851, D 826
Dazzling Daisy p.16	A 54m (60yd), B 90m (99yd), C 234m (256yd), D 468m (512yd), E 288m (315yd)	A 180m (197yd), B 300m (329yd), C 780m (854yd), D 1560m (1707yd), E 960m (1050yd)	A 315m (345yd), B 525m (575yd), C 1365m (1493yd), D 2730m (2986yd), E 1680m (1838yd)	A 914a, B 825, C 851, D 1971, E 1967
Granny's Corner p.18	A 54m (60yd), B 342m (375yd), C 72m (79yd), D 288m (315yd), E 108m (119yd), F 126m (138yd), G 144m (158yd)	A 180m (197yd), B 1140m (1247yd), C 240m (263yd), D 960m (1050yd), E 360m (394yd (394yd), F 420m (460yd), G 480m (525yd)	A 315m (345yd), B 1995m (2182yd), C 420m (460yd), D 1680m (1838yd), E 630m (689yd), F 735m (804yd), G 840m (919yd)	A 825, B 808, C 820, D 887, E 849, F 896, G 1986
Interrupted p.20	A 468m (512yd), B 108m (119yd), C 72m (79yd), D 252m (276yd), E 252m (276yd)	A 1560m (1707yd), B 360m (394yd), C 240m (263yd), D 840m (919yd), E 840m (919yd)	A 2730m (2986yd), B 630m (689yd), C 420m (460yd), D 1470m (1608yd), E 1470m (1608yd)	A 1973, B 816, C 1952, D 887, E 903
Log Cabin p.22	A 72m (79yd), B 90m (99yd), C 126m (138yd), D 162m (178yd), E 198m (217yd), F 324m (355yd), G 396m (434yd)	A 240m (263yd), B 300m (329yd), C 420m (460yd), D 540m (591yd), E 660m (722yd), F 1080m (1182yd), G 1320m (1444yd)	A 420m (460yd), B 525m (575yd), C 735m (804yd), D 945m (1034yd), E 1155m (1264yd), F 1890m (2067yd), G 2310m (2527yd)	A 1921, B 820, C 851, D 827, E 849, F 903, G 848

Pattern	Baby blanket	Throw	Bedspread	Cascade colours
Holi Festival Blanket p.24	Ch113; repeats = 36 wide x 5 high; A–L 68m (75yd) each	Ch185; repeats = 60 wide x 10 high; A–L 225m (247yd) each	Ch257; repeats = 84 wide x 12 high; A–L 378m (414yd) each	A 885, B 844, C 887, D 820, E 825, F 807, G 1921, H 871, I 851, J 1952, K 847, L 875
Neon Frills p.28	Ch184; repeats = 90 wide x 30 high; A 973m (1065yd), B–D 162m (178yd) each	Ch306; repeats = 151 wide x 60 high; A 3317m (1628yd), B–D 544m (595yd) each	Ch428; repeats = 212 wide x 74 high; A 5801m (6345yd), B–D 916m (1002yd) each	A 816, B 1973, C 1952, D 851
Pastel Rows p.30	A–D 180m (197yd) each, E 324m (355yd)	A–D 600m (657yd) each, E 1080m (1182yd)	A–D 1050m (1149yd) each, E 1080m (1182yd)	A 1967, B 850, C 875, D 897, E 901
Reversi p.32	A 72m (79yd), B 144m (158yd), C 216m (237yd), D 288m (315yd), E 360m (394yd), F 432m (473yd)	A 240m (263yd), B 480m (525yd), C 720m (788yd), D 960m (1050yd), E 1200m (1313yd), F 1440m (1575yd)	A 420m (460yd), B 840m (919yd), C 1260m (1378yd), D 1680m (1838yd), E 2100m (2297yd), F 2520m (2756yd)	A 817, B 1915, C 1941, D 1940, E 903, F 807
Rice Field p.34	Ch122; repeats = 60 wide x 30 high; A–D 363m (397yd) each	Ch204; repeats = 101 wide x 61 high; A–D 1239m (1355yd) each	Ch286; repeats = 142 wide x 76 high; A–D 2166m (2369yd) each	A 887, B 1971, C 228, D 807
Textured Ripple p.36	Ch124; repeats = 30 wide x 8 high; A–G 258m (283yd) each	Ch208; repeats = 51 wide x 16 high; A–G 878m (961yd) each	Ch288; repeats = 71 wide x 20 high; A–G 1527m (1670yd) each	A 825, B 834, C 914a, D 1967, E 844, F 1973, G 850
Carnival p.38	Ch116; repeats = 11 wide x 11 high; A, C, E, G 177m (194yd) each, B, D, F 178m (195yd) each	Ch196; repeats = 19 wide x 22 high; A, C, E, G 628m (687yd) each, B, D, F 629m (688yd) each	Ch266; repeats = 26 wide x 28 high; A, C, E, G 1117m (1222yd) each, B, D, F 1118m (1223yd) each	A 810, B 851, C 825, D 903, E 807, F 1967, G 1971
Checkmate p.40	Ch121; repeats = 6 wide x 6 high; A–B 432m (473yd) each	Ch201; repeats = 10 wide x 12 high; A–B 1440m (1575yd) each	Ch281; repeats = 14 wide x 15 high; A–B 2520m (2756yd) each	A 848, B 820
Diagonals Baby Blanket p.42	A 126m (138yd), B 612m (670yd), C 576m (630yd), D 126m (138yd)	A 420m (460yd), B 2040m (2231yd), C 1920m (2100yd), D 420m (460yd)	A 735m (804yd), B 3570m (3905yd), C 3360m (3675yd), D 735m (804yd)	A 1952, B 871, C 849, D 877
Coral Shells p.46	Ch114; repeats = 18 wide x 6 high; A 171m (188yd), B 141m (155yd), C 250m (274yd), D 193m (212yd), E 196m (215yd)	Ch186; repeats = 30 wide x 12 high; A 566m (619yd), B 462m (506yd), C 817m (894yd), D 632m (692yd), E 639m (699yd)	Ch258; repeats = 42 wide x 15 high; A 989m (1082yd), B 805m (881yd), C 1419m (1552yd), D 1100m (1203yd), E 2079m (2274yd)	A 874, B 901, C 1973, D 827, E 1942
Strawberries and Cream p.48	A 522m (571yd), B 666m (729yd)	A 1740m (1903yd), B 2220m (2428yd)	A 3045m (3331yd), B 3885m (4249yd)	A 910a, B 1922
Fizzy Mint p.50	A 180m (197yd), B 252m (276yd), C 342m (375yd), D 252m (276yd)	A 600m (657yd), B 840m (919yd), C 1140m (1247yd), D 840m (919yd)	A 1050m (1149yd), B 1470m (1608yd), C 1995m (2182yd), D 1470m (1608yd)	A 834, B 817, C 227, D 850

Pattern	Baby blanket	Throw	Bedspread	Cascade colours
Granny Stripes p.52	Ch113; repeats = 36 wide x 5 high; A 261m (286yd), B–D 245m (268yd) each, E 61m (67yd)	Ch185; repeats = 60 wide x 9 high; A 774m (847yd), B–D 723m (791yd) each, E 181m (198yd)	Ch260; repeats = 85 wide x 12 high; A 1350m (1477yd), B–D 1264m (1383yd) each, E 315m (345yd)	A 814, B 227, C 887, D 821, E 808
Lily Pad p.54	A 54m (60yd), B 144m (158yd), C 126m (138yd), D 198m (217yd), E 234m (256yd), F 162m (178yd)	A 180m (197yd), B 480m (525yd), C 420m (460yd), D 660m (722yd), E 780m (854yd), F 540m (591yd)	A 315m (345yd), B 840m (919yd), C 735m (804yd), D 1155m (1264yd), E 135m (1493yd), F 945m (1034yd)	A 901, B 1921, C 817, D 887, E 802, F 1985
Luxor p.56	A 324m (355yd), B 90m (99yd), C 162m (178yd), D 216m (237yd), E 270m (296yd)	A 1080m (1182yd), B 300m (329yd), C 540m (591yd), D 720m (788yd), E 900m (985yd)	A 1890m (2067yd), B 525m (575yd), C 945m (1034yd), D 1260m (1378yd), E 1575m (1723yd)	A 825, B 802, C 887, D 844, E 1971
Phoenix p.58	A 54m (60yd), B 90m (99yd), C 144m (158yd), D 216m (237yd), E 450m (493yd)	A 180m (197yd), B 300m (329yd), C 480m (525yd), D 720m (788yd), E 1500m (1641yd)	A 315m (345yd), B 525m (575yd), C 840m (919yd), D 1260m (1378yd), E 2625m (2871yd)	A 808, B 821, C 1952, D 892, E 816
Granny Quilt p.60	18 blocks (3 rows of 6 blocks); A 90m (99yd), B 162m (178yd), C 198m (217yd), D 216m (237yd), E 243m (266yd), F 261m (286yd)	60 blocks (5 rows of 12 blocks); A 300m (329yd), B 540m (591yd), C 660m (722yd), D 720m (788yd), E 810m (886yd), F 870m (952yd)	105 blocks (7 rows of 15 blocks); A 525m (575yd), B 945m (1034yd), C 1155m (1264yd), D 1260m (1378yd), E 1418m (1551yd), F 1523m (1666yd)	A 820, B 834, C 914a, D 851, E 842, F 1986
Purplicious p.64	Ch134; repeats = 26 wide x 5 high; A 693m (758yd), B–F 611m (669yd) each	Ch224; repeats = 44 wide x 10 high; A 2286m (2500yd), B–F 201m (220yd) each	Ch309; repeats = 61 wide x 12 high; A 3824m (4182yd), B–F 335m (367yd) each	A 1986, B 850, C 901, D 849, E 820, F 1952
Bobble Band p.66	Ch149; repeats = 36 wide x 9 high; A 596m (652yd), B 133m (146yd), C 364m (399yd), D 133m (146yd)	Ch245; repeats = 60 wide x 18 high; A 1969m (2154yd), B 438m (480yd), C 1207m (1320yd), D 438m (480yd)	Ch350; repeats = 85 wide x 23 high; A 3591m (3928yd), B 799m (874yd), C 2206m (2413yd), D 799m (874yd)	A 834, B 1942, C 910a, D 816
Bibbledy Bobbledy Blue p.68	Ch125; repeats = 30 wide x 5 high; A 422m (462yd), B 62m (68yd), C 123m (135yd), D 121m (133yd)	Ch205; repeats = 50 wide x 10 high; A 1403m (1535yd), B 203m (223yd), C 406m (445yd), D 399m (437yd)	Ch289; repeats = 71 wide x 12 high; A 2389m (2613yd), B 345m (378yd), C 689m (754yd), D 678m (742yd)	A 847, B 820, C 903, D 851
Crossed Hatch p.70	Ch93; repeats = 45 wide x 7 high; A–E 155m (170yd) each	Ch153; repeats = 75 wide x 15 high; A–E 486m (532yd) each	Ch215; repeats = 106 wide x 19 high; A–E 854m (934yd) each	A 896, B 914a, C 827, D 1967, E 850
Flower Patch p.72	A 144m (158yd), B–E 216m (237yd) each, F 720m (788yd)	A 480m (525yd), B–E 720m (788yd) each, F 2400m (2625yd)	A 840m (919yd), B–E 1260m (1378yd) each, F 4200m (4594yd)	A 825, B 836, C 1941, D 1915, E 842, F 227
Folk Flower p.74	A–C 216m (237yd) each, D 306m (335yd), E 594m (650yd)	A–C 720m (788yd) each, D 1020m (1116yd), E 1980m (2166yd)	A–C 1260m (1378yd) each, D 1785m (1953yd), E 3465m (3790yd)	A 820, B 1952, C 851, D 914a, E 848
Knotty but Nice p.76	A 90m (99yd), B 216m (237yd), C 234m (256yd), D 180m (197yd), E 252m (276yd)	A 300m (329yd), B 720m (788yd), C 780m (854yd), D 600m (657yd), E 840m (919yd)	A 525m (575yd), B 1260m (1378yd), C 1365m (1493yd), D 1050m (1149yd), E 1470m (1608yd)	A 825, B 914a, C 1973, D 844, E 842

Pattern	Baby blanket	Throw	Bedspread	Cascade colours
Roisin Baby Blanket p.78	A 108m (119yd), B 216m (237yd), C 612m (670yd), D–G 234m (256yd) each	A 360m (394yd), B 720m (788yd), C 2040m (2231yd), D–G 3120m (3413yd) each	A 630m (689yd), B 1260m (1378yd), C 3570m (3905yd), D–G 5460m (5972yd) each	A 851, B 820, C 871, D 1967, E 903, F 834, G 1973
Pond p.82	Ch130; repeats = 18 wide x 4 high; A 278m (305yd), B 113m (124yd), C 113m (124yd), D 76m (84yd), E 91m (100yd), F 152m (167yd)	Ch214; repeats = 30 wide x 7 high; A 813m (891yd), B 327m (358yd), C 327m (358yd), D 219m (240yd), E 267m (292yd), F 440m (482yd)	Ch298; repeats = 42 wide x 9 high; A 1462m (1599yd), B 588m (644yd), C 588m (644yd), D 394m (431yd), E 477m (522yd), F 790m (864yd)	A 810, B 802, C 887, D 821, E 871, F 885
Snakes and Ladders p.84	Ch112; repeats = 18 wide x 6 high; A–C 144m (158yd) each, D 217m (238yd), E 157m (172yd), F 88m (97yd)	Ch184; repeats = 30 wide x 12 high; A–C 478m (523yd) each, D 722m (790yd), E 535m (586yd), F 290m (318yd)	Ch256; repeats = 42 wide x 15 high; A–C 835m (914yd) each, D 1263m (1382yd), E 935m (1023yd), F 507m (555yd)	A 814, B 1986, C 808, D 871, E 802, F 1952
Tile p.86	A 828m (906yd), B 396m (434yd)	A 2760m (3019yd), B 1320m (1444yd)	A 4830m (5283yd), B 2310m (2527yd)	A 901, B 871
Tulips p.88	A 396m (434yd), B 288m (315yd), C 126m (138yd), D 396m (434yd)	120 blocks (10 blocks x 12 rows) A 1320m (1444yd), B 960m (1050yd), C 420m (460yd), D 1320m (1444yd)	A 2310m (2527yd), B 1680m (1838yd), C 735m (804yd), D 2310m (2527yd)	A 814, B 887, C 836, D 1921
Wavy p.90	Ch128; repeats = 8 wide x 6 high; A–C 135m (148yd) each, D 220m (242yd), E 219m (240yd)	Ch212; repeats = 14 wide x 12 high; A–C 552m (604yd) each, D 758m (829yd), E 754m (825yd)	Ch296; repeats = 20 wide x 15 high; A–C 967m (1058yd) each, D 1344m (1470yd), E 1340m (1466yd)	A 887, B 807, C 848, D 871, E 808
Purple Petal Eater p.92	A 342m (375yd), B 360m (394yd), C 126m (138yd), D 666m (729yd)	A 1140m (1247yd), B 1200m (1313yd), C 420m (460yd), D 2220m (2428yd)	A 1995m (2182yd), B 2100m (2297yd), C 735m (804yd), D 3885m (4249yd)	A 1942, B 834, C 903, D 1971
Sideways p.94	Ch129; repeats = 30 wide x 10 high; A–F 152m (167yd) each	Ch209; repeats = 50 wide x 20 high; A–F 500m (547yd) each	Ch293; repeats = 71 wide x 25 high; A–F 882m (965yd) each	A 875, B 834, C 1973, D 871, E 1942, F 825
Spiky Waves Throw p.96	Ch122; repeats = 12 wide x 5 high; A–G 240m (263yd) each	Ch202; repeats = 20 wide x 9 high; A–G 720m (788yd) each	Ch282; repeats = 28 wide x 11 high; A–G 1232m (348yd) each	A 901, B 807, C 804, D 844, E 227, F 1942, G 1915

Edging colours

- **Knitty p.104** A 825, B 851, C 842
- **Curvy p.104** A 901, B 820
- **Spikes p.105** A 901
- **Crab p.105** A 851
- **Arches p.105** A 847

- **Mosaic p.106** A 842, B 901, C 847, D 851, E 820, F 825, G 808
- **Fancy p.106** A 901, B 847, C 851, D 825
- **Flounce p.107** A 825, B 851, C 901
- **Flowery p.107** A 825

- **Ruffled p.108** A 820, B 901, C 808, D 842
- **Granny p.109** A 851, B 901, C 808
- **Prism p.109** A 901, B 842, C 847, D 851

Index

Credits

To Sean, my partner and best friend. Thanks for turning a blind eye to the mountains of yarn and the pile of crochet that's constantly on the sofa in the exact spot you want to sit. The end – nae mair.

Thanks to all the folks at Quarto for being great to work with as always. Particularly thanks to Emma Clayton for colour-lust adjustments and Michelle Pickering for being the best and most eagle-eyed of editors.

And Ubuntu. Saved my files again!

www.leoniemorgan.com

All photographs and illustrations are the copyright of Quarto Publishing plc. While every effort has been made to credit contributors, Quarto would like to apologise should there have been any omissions or errors – and would be pleased to make the appropriate correction for future editions of the book.

With special thanks to Cascade Yarns for providing the yarns used in this book. See page 124 for details of colours used.

www.cascadeyarns.com